D1565285

Eighteen Texts

EIGHTEEN TEXTS

Writings by Contemporary Greek Authors

EDITED BY WILLIS BARNSTONE

1972 HARVARD UNIVERSITY PRESS

CAMBRIDGE, MASSACHUSETTS

Acknowledgment. The assistance of Classic Book Associates,
in bringing about the English-language edition of this work
is gratefully acknowledged.

But Goddess, I cannot hear your voice.

—DIONYSIOS SOLOMOS, "The Free Beseiged"

The Editor wishes to dedicate this book to
Christopher Janus, who has labored for the
restoration of democracy in Greece   W.B.

Preface

In presenting original literary works for the first time in three years, we are contributing to an attempt to focus again on the problem of the Greek writer under present-day conditions.

The repeal of prepublication censorship is not enough to bring about the intellectual emancipation of a land when major vital areas are still surrounded by complex pressures that do not allow them to develop fully. Nevertheless, after mature consideration we wish to repeat, or rather to emphasize—each in his own way—our belief in some fundamental values: first among them is the right of free intellectual and artistic expression, which we will not stop claiming, and which is tied inextricably to a respect for the dignity and opinions not only of each creative artist but of each man.

This collective volume underscores the common beliefs and demands, which unite us beyond differences of attitude and style.

We think it appropriate to place first, in the position of honor, a poem by George Seferis, published in other countries but unpublished in his own tongue.

Contents

Foreword   *by Cedric Whitman*

> When the day of slavery overtakes a man,
> Zeus robs him of half his worth.

With today's artists there is always, as with Homer, the inevitable
quest for the central substance in human life. Homer composed some
two centuries before actual democracy was born in Greece, but he
knew the precept: Only a free man is a whole man. Freedom is of
the mind, and when articulate men are driven to assert that fact it
is because some external force has befallen them, a tyranny that drives
their words into the mind's refuge and their pens into dangerous
utterance.

These documents come from members of the aristocracy of the mind.
They know of danger, but they know best of the whole man, and
the need for him. A whole man is always fierce, never violent. His
cowardly hypostases in tyranny have been tried, cheerfully and vainly,
in many a country; the peerless Spanish poet Garcia Lorca, for instance, went to a firing squad and an unmarked grave. The soldiers
probably had no idea who he was. Now everyone knows. After the
harm is done, the world wakes up.

In such periods, poets, essayists, story writers have much to lose,
such as life or freedom; but these are giving what Greece has always
had to give—individuality, and the love of man. There have been

Cedric Whitman

better times, when Greek writers found their task in seeking words
for expansive understanding rather than for political infighting. It will
change.

When texts, so called, perform a ceremonial function, they become
not merely texts; they are testimonies. One, in fact, is so entitled.
They do not pose the aesthetic problem of the correct literary mode
for a given era, a problem once so neatly settled in antiquity by the
Hellenistic poets. They arise from a more desperate questioning: how
to say anything in a time when speech is obscured, language prescribed,
and meaning manacled? They are all moving; all proclaim the long-
lived Hellenic necessity of communication between man and man,
while recognizing the imperiled state of such communication now. The
styles are various. One passes from the decorum of Seferis' tragic vision,
through the desperate quest for faith in Spiros Plaskovitis' *Radar*, to
the nightmares of Sinopoulos' poem and the ghastly pirate raid by
Menis Koumandareas or the surrealistic *Actor* by Takis Koufopoulos.

It is unnecessary to run through the table of contents or estimate
in advance what must be read to be realized. Literary value is of
secondary importance to the circumstance under which these documents were written. They come from a world where fake morality
is publicly mouthed, and truth, if it can be spoken at all, is spoken
in whispers. They are testimonies from a nation eclipsed by a puny
minority, a minority disgracefully supported by the very world power
that produced highhearted Philhellenes in 1821, many of whose bodies
are buried in the Heroes' Precinct in Missolonghi. There also the heart
of Byron lies, centered amid monuments to many other lovers of Greece
who came from all parts of Europe, with piety in their hearts and
valor in their hands. These texts are the testimonies of a new generation of lovers of Greece, where the concept of democratic freedom,
twice established, is now momentarily interred.

But democracy is hard to bury. There are skilled morticians of
course, inhumanly self-interested, ready for any crime, from torture
and murder to a ban on Sophocles' *Antigone*. They forget. In the
old ballad, the young hero Constantine, though long buried, burst out
of his grave to keep a promise that he had given. When he had fulfilled
it he went back to his grave, for there also he had a promise to keep.

Foreword

This poem vividly dramatizes what has always been the ethical triad
of Greek culture—truth, freedom, and death. If the first two sound
like vague abstractions, the third is concrete enough; it gives body,
or at least bones, to the others. Greece keeps her promises. These poems
and stories show that the faith is still kept, and that we may still
suffer, yet survive, tomorrow.

In Greece, the cat is a fierce animal. Seldom domesticated, it is
a fighter, and it is no wonder that the legend arose that legions of
them slew poisonous snakes on a famous promontory of Cyprus. They
suffered from the poison; many died; but the others, well fed by the
good monks of Saint Nicholas, destroyed the snakes who had taken the
place of the human population. There are some legitimately dangerous
snakes in Greece; but when they displace humanity, and take on ex-
ternally human form, somewhere out of the great legend, the myth
of Greece herself, one hears the ringing of the bell of Saint Nicholas
summoning the cats to food in the evening, and in the morning to
battle, with snakes. Hideous as that fight may be, it is better than
becoming a Plaster Cast.

These texts are a warning, not because any of the authors poses
a conspiratorial threat, but because all are committed to a Greece that
is free. They constitute a reminder of what Greece has always insisted
on being; but in such a celebration of Hellenic fire, there is danger.
When Archbishop Germanos raised the flag of revolution in 1821,
he must have foreseen the bloodshed to follow. By contrast, we have
here an intermediate statement, better, a question, from men who are
not men of destruction to men who are; their question is, simply,
what can or must be said in answer to your actions? The texts, as
they stand, are singularly controlled expressions of a dilemma, and
the only point of this note is to make explicit what is implied in their
sorrowful pages. They ask for reading, understanding, in the terrible
foreknowledge that, in time, that other great Philhellene, Shelley, will
burst his grave, like Constantine, to keep his promise, and call again:

Rise like lions after slumber
In unvanquishable number . . .
Ye are many, they are few.

Introduction   *by Stratis Haviaras*

The restrictions imposed on freedom of expression in Greece since the 1967 military takeover were aimed at everyone, particularly the intellecutals. Because of these restrictions, during the past four and a half years, many artists, writers, and educators chose to go into exile; because of violations of these restrictions many others were thrown into prison. When *Eighteen Texts* appeared in Athens in the summer of 1970, it signaled the resumption, under a totalitarian regime, of the cultural ferment that paralleled the political liberalization of Greece in the early sixties. Although the military government lifted the preventive censorship that year, it was still very dangerous to challenge its policies regarding freedom of thought and of the press. Unlike other protest literature concerning the situation in Greece, *Eighteen Texts* is testimony from within. It was designed to operate publicly and directly under the thumb of an oppressive system, rather than privately or abroad.

The volume marks an abrupt change in the stance of the Greek intellectuals. They had been silent since the military putsch of April 1967. They had written but not published, refusing to submit their works to the censor—thus severing their means of communication with each other and the public. In a way their silence served the regime,

which in the process of "re-educating" the Greek people was closing
down or merging schools, dismissing teachers, installing military
watchdogs in the universities, re-emphasizing the Katharevousa
("purist") language, and introducing new textbooks to create "faithful
citizens." Finally the Greek intellectuals realized that if they remained
aloof, the damage could reach unimaginable proportions. So they proceeded from protest by silence to subversion by creative activity. *Eighteen Texts* and several underground publications that preceded it by
a few months indicated that the Greeks knew how to protect the blos-
soming of their letters. Today, more than a year after the appearance
of this work, all literary activity points to the start of a new period
of enlightenment, similar to that which bred revolutionary ferment
in Greece at the end of the eighteenth century.

Eighteen Texts gives a good view of the present state of Greek letters.
Its four poems, three essays, one travelogue, and ten pieces of fiction
are representative of some of the best writing from the latest stage
in the evolution of twentieth-century Greek literature.

George Seferis' contribution to Greek letters began in the 1930's.
The day of Cavafy, whose work had remained outside the mainstream
of Greek literature, was coming to a close. And Kostis Palamas, who
had dominated Greek poetry, became less reluctant to allow other
voices to be heard. A new generation could start to experiment. With
compositions such as "Erotikos Logos," "The Cistern," and "Mythis-
torima" Seferis began to give a new direction to Greek poetry, which
was bound to become, in his words, "more condensed, elliptical, difficult." The poet's need for a literary mythology drew him to mythical
and historical figures and episodes—but only in a pattern dictated
by the other, stronger element in his poetry: the world of the present.
Long a career diplomat, Seferis refrained from obvious political themes
in his writings and avoided any public expression in commentary or
action. But as conditions in Greece led to the April 1967 crisis, and
as military rule persisted, Seferis could not remain silent. In the spring
of 1969 he made available to the international press a statement, "Toward a Precipice," in which he condemned the dictatorship and asked
for an end to oppression. The regime responded with a vicious attack
on him, both as individual and as poet. Seferis refused to engage in

xvi

a verbal exchange with the junta, but a few months later there appeared, in England, a translation of "The Cats of Saint Nicholas," whose Greek version, a year later, was given the place of honor at the beginning of *Eighteen Texts*. At the end of this poem, Seferis uses an excerpt from a 1580 document about Cyprus as an allegory of the extinction of the Greeks—the race that fought for ages against the dark forces of the world.

Another poet is Takis Sinopoulos, whose work entitled "The Ballad of Ioanna and Constantinos" was hailed as a major contribution at the time of its publication in 1961. "Nights," five interconnected pieces from a longer poem, is filled with tragic testimonies from various stations in the passion of Greece, in the perspective of recent history. The poem reads very much like a film script. Sudden, powerful images, descriptions of interrogation and of shadowy encounters in a city under occupation, brief exchanges, and recurring names of men marked by death, make this poem less subjectively lyrical. Whether directly participating, or through the senses of a persona, Sinopoulos retains a strong emotional involvement in the poetic episode, without relinquishing his role as critical observer.

"The Target" of Manolis Anagnostakis is virtually the new state of affairs in Greece under the military regime. It is a series of fourteen short poems, each depicting a certain aspect of this "new reality" and its consequent manifestations. As in Sinopoulos' poem, there are frequent references to Greece's recent past. In his free verse, Anagnostakis retains a subdued, conversational tone, avoiding the excessive as well as the abstract. Anagnostakis, a man of liberal beliefs, has been a rigorous critic of the easy political message delivered by some writers in the name of socialist realism.

The fourth poetry text in this volume, "Traffic Lights" by Lina Kasdaglis, is a brief, lyrical piece in free verse, one rather simple in its symbolism. It transmits the emotion with which the poet observes the "nameless person" who contemplates getting to the "other side" but who is not allowed or is unable to cross the street.

Nora Anagnostakis' essay, "A Testimony," explains why she failed to write the essay she had originally planned. That essay would have begun with this thought: "In the kingdom of the mute, only a poetry

of gestures will flower; the criticism of that poetry will be a criticism
of pantomime." But that essay required words that were "absolutely
concrete, stripped of allegory, symbol, satire, myths—all those devices
which literature, even in better days, uses freely to enrich—but not
smother—expression." Obviously such an essay could not be completed
under the circumstances, and, if it were, the author could not possibly
print it. "For those whose gestures are too 'poetic,' there are always
laws and authorities to bind or cut off their hands." The other authors
in this volume have, in varying degrees, used allegory, symbols, satire,
and myth as integral elements of style, but they have also used them,
together with gestures, to express all that could not be said directly.
In this context Nora Anagnostakis' apologia provides ample information regarding the dilemma confronting the Greek writer at work.

D. N. Maronitis, author of "Arrogance and Intoxication," was an
associate professor of classical Greek literature at the university of
Salonika. In January 1968 he was dismissed, and in December
1970, a few months after the appearance of *Eighteen Texts*, he was
arrested on charges of participating in "subversive activities." He was
held in prison for eleven months without trial, then released. Maronitis
was neither the first nor the last educator to lose his job or to be
imprisoned. Today, according to an Athens daily newspaper, over one
hundred teaching positions in Greek universities remain vacant, mainly
as a result of similar government action. Maronitis' essay is a brilliant
analysis of C. P. Cavafy's "Darius," a poem dealing with the creative
man and the impact on his work of adverse social upheavals.
Maronitis is concerned ostensibly with a commentary on the poet's
work, but in fact he actively urges others to use a language of signals,
the "prisoners' language."

Language and *its* prisoners is the subject of Alexandros Arghyriou's
essay. "The Style of a Language and the Language of a Style" deals
with one of Greece's most perplexing problems, affecting the transmis-
sion of knowledge to the people. The problem of language has been
frustrating the Greeks for the past hundred and fifty years. There
is Demotic, the living language of the people, in which literature is
written—a language that evolved from ancient Greek. And there is
Katharevousa, a language that was literally manufactured in order

to bridge centuries of foreign domination and provide the new nation
with an awareness of "the glory that was Greece." It was Katharevousa
that became Greece's official language, a status confirmed by constitu-
tional amendment in 1911. Despite continuous movements for its ban-
ishment from the schools and other official institutions which are its
main strongholds, the situation remains unchanged. Efforts for the
adoption of Demotic have paralleled broader efforts for social, political,
and educational reform, just as the reintroduction or protection of
Katharevousa has paralleled counterefforts by the Greek right and their
foreign patrons to preserve the status quo. Since the military takeover
in April 1967, new emphasis has been placed by the government on
the use of Katharevousa. Arghyriou's thorough historical and critical
account helps familiarize the reader with the essence of the language
problem in Greece.

Nikos Kasdaglis' "Athos," a diary entry about a visit to the Holy
Mountain two months after the military coup, reflects the author's
desire to heal or reinforce a wounded faith. An early center of Greek
Orthodox Christianity, Athos, an autonomous republic within Greece,
has been subjected to stricter control by the military regime. First
inhabited around 850, this promontory on the Chalcidice peninsula
still houses some two thousand orthodox monks in its twenty monasteries, and includes among its treasures some of the most important
examples of Byzantine iconography, plus a vast quantity of classical
and medieval manuscripts.

Fiction, represented by ten texts, occupies the largest portion of this
volume. Four of these are short stories, set in Spain or Latin American
"republics." The shift in locale enabled the authors to attack the political situation in Greece without naming it outright. In spite of foreign
or fictional names of place or character and the fact that all repressive
regimes have common characteristics, the stories are genuinely Greek.
Terror, bitterness, compassion, and hope fill these texts, whose authors
rank among the most able writers in Greece today.

Kay Ciceleis is known for novels and stories written in English and
in Greek. Her best known work, *The Way to Colonos,* is a modern
triptych based on ancient Greek tragedies. In *Eighteen Texts* she is
represented with "Brief Dialogue," a story depicting a cautiously con-

ducted political conversation between a taxicab driver and his passenger—a very familiar scene in Greece.

Rodis Roufos, author of "The Candidate," has written several novels, of which *The Age of Bronze*, is based on the Cypriot struggle for liberation. Mr. Roufos is a leading figure in the growing literary-political oppositon to the regime.

T. D. Frangopoulos, author of "El Procurador," has written fiction, criticism, and drama but is mainly known for his poetry. He has published five collections of verse, and has been praised for his clarity of language and craftsmanship. His poetry has been considered that of humanism, a reflection of the conscience of our time.

Stratis Tsirkas, author of "Weatherchange," has written many books, among them *Cavafy and His Times* and a trilogy, *Ungoverned Cities*, a milestone in contemporary Greek literature.

When *Eighteen Texts* came out in Athens, Spiros Plaskovitis, author of "The Radar," was a political prisoner on the island of Aegina. It may well be that the story was written in prison, for its circumstances offer a parallel to the prisoner-guard theme. Here again is the presence of the military, here again the question of faith.

"Going Home" by Alexandros Kotzias, is a chapter from an unpublished novel. It deals with men in uniform, their mentality and concerns, versus the "other people," mainly the young with their own lives and aspirations. "Going Home" represents a newer, terser, more dynamic style of writing in the postwar prose of Greece. These qualities are present even in Mr. Kotzias' first published work, *Siege*, a novel about the civil strife in Greece during the Nazi occupation.

Menis Koumandareas, the second-youngest fiction writer in this volume, participates with "Holy Sunday on the Rock," an excerpt from a longer, unpublished story. This magnificent piece relates the invasion of a sea town and the massacre of its population by pirates. The scene is reconstructed as though from an old chronicle, or from the logbook of a passing ship whose captain has witnessed it through his spyglass. Seen from that distance, the massacre is no more than a seventeenth-century popular theater production performed by troupes of actors improvising on prearranged synopses with formalized characters.

The remaining stories are indicative, in varying degrees, of the new

directions in which contemporary Greek fiction may develop. Raised
in a period suspicious of the formulas and styles of prewar prose,
these representatives of the new generation of writers are almost obsessed with what may be called a fantasy whose function is to expose
reality to a frightening degree. Whether or not the concept owes its
origins to surrealist experience in Greek poetry, or was suggested by
the realities of the times we live in, it is too soon to tell. The reader
must judge whether what seems here to be surreal, absurd, or symbolic
exaggeration is justified—and why.

Thanasis Valtinos' story, "The Plaster Cast," is based entirely on
a metaphor frequently used by Colonel Papadopoulos to justify the
military coup and later the prolongation of martial law. Greece, he
would say, was in grave danger. We had to operate. Now she is in
a cast—in satisfactory condition. But she must remain in the cast.
Indefinitely . . . until she is completely well. Valtinos' story is written
in the first person; as it is he, the author, who is put in the cast,
metaphor becomes personal experience.

Takis Koufopoulos wrote "The Actor" in 1966, a year before the
coup. He successfully depicts the confusion in Greece following
the ouster of George Papandreou and his cabinet on July 15, 1965.
The actor, who is also part-time director in the theatrical production
in this story, reminds one of young King Constantine in 1965 and
1966. When, during the confusion on stage the curtain suddenly falls,
the surprised actor tries to make his way out from the proscenium;
but as soon as he parts one layer of curtains he finds another separating
him from his audience, then another, and still another. Trapped in
a maze of curtains, the actor may never lose his title but will soon
lose his audience.

George Himonas, the youngest author in this volume, has indicated
with four short published novels that writing like his may effect radical
changes in Greek prose. Although only the first three "cycles" of *Dr.
Ineotis* are included in *Eighteen Texts,* the presence of several unique
qualities in the writing of Himonas is unmistakable. *Dr. Ineotis* is
a dark, merciless story, with compact, powerful descriptions and an
imagery that brings to mind Kafka and Goya, Apocalypse and science
fiction.

Stratis Haviaras

It is a shuddering coincidence that the oldest author, George Seferis, and the youngest, George Himonas, are both haunted with the same frightening vision: the extinction of the Greek people, or worse, of their humanity.

Cambridge, Massachusetts
December 1971

Eighteen Texts

The Cats of Saint Nicholas   GEORGE SEFERIS

But deep inside me sings
the Fury's lyreless threnody:
my heart, self-taught, has lost
the precious confidence of hope . . .
    —Aeschylus, *Agamemnon*

"That's the Cape of Cats ahead," the captain said to me,
pointing out a low stretch of shore in the fog,
the beach deserted; it was Christmas day—
". . . and in the distance toward the West the wave gave birth to
    Aphrodite;
they call the place the Greek's Rock.
Left ten degrees rudder!"
She had Salome's eyes, the cat I lost a year ago;
and old Ramazan, how he would look death square in the eyes,
whole days long in the snow of the East,
under the frozen sun,
days long square in the eyes: the young hearth god.
Don't stop, traveler.
"Left ten degrees rudder," mumbled the helmsman.

. . . maybe my friend was close by,

1

George Seferis

now between ships,
shut up in a small house with pictures,
searching for windows behind the frames.
The ship's bell struck
like a coin from some city that disappeared
coming to revive in the mind, as it falls,
alms from another time.

"It's strange," the captain said,
"That bell—given what day it is—
reminded me of the other, the monastery bell.
A monk told me the story,
a half-mad monk, a kind of dreamer.

"It was the time of the great drought,
forty years without rain,
the whole island devastated,
people died and snakes were born.
This cape had millions of snakes
thick as a man's leg
and full of poison.
In those days the monastery of St. Nicholas
was held by the monks of St. Basil,
and they couldn't work their fields
and they couldn't put their flocks to pasture;
in the end they were saved by the cats they raised.
Every day at dawn a bell would strike
and the crew of cats would move out to battle.
They'd fight the day long, until
the bell would sound the evening feed.
Supper done, the bell would sound again
and out they'd go to fight the night's war.
They say it was a wonderful thing to see them,
some lame, some twisted, others missing
a nose, an ear, their hides in shreds.
So to the sound of four bells a day

2

months went by, years, season after season.
Wildly obstinate, always wounded,
they annihilated the snakes; but in the end they disappeared:
they just couldn't take in that much poison.
Like a sunken ship
they didn't leave a thing behind them on the surface:
no meow, no bell even.
Steady as you go!
                    What could the poor devils do,
fighting like that day and night, drinking in
the poisonous blood of those reptiles?
Centuries of poison; generations of poison."
"Steady as you go," echoed the indifferent helmsman.

translated by Edmund Keeley

   See, among other travelers between 1483 and 1750, Estienne de Lusignan,
Description de toute l'isle de Cypre (Paris, 1580; Ammochostos: Les éditions l'oiseau,
1968): "So as not to forget how these poisonous reptiles were exterminated from
the above-mentioned promontory, one must note the following: . . . the first Duke
of Cyprus had a monastery built for monks of the order of Saint Basil in honor of
Saint Nicholas, and he gave this whole promontory to the monastery on condition
that the monks would be bound to feed at least one hundred cats every day, for which
they would provide some daily meat in the morning and the evening, at the sound
of a small bell, so that the cats would not feed on venom alone, and for the rest of
the day and the night would hunt down these serpents. Even in our time this
monastery fed more than forty cats. And thence comes its name, even to this day:
the Promontory of the Cats."—G.S.

Brief Dialogue   KAY CICELLIS

A busy time on the avenue; traffic almost at a standstill. It was
late afternoon; the light thickened slowly, like honey, and slowly the
wide stream of cars moved toward the heart of the city.

In a taxi two men, caught in the slow stream: driver and passenger.
They waited in silence for the solid mass of vehicles to start moving
again.

The passenger had hailed the taxi a few blocks up the avenue, just
off a small quiet square planted with acacias. Before getting in, he
had hesitated; then with a decided look he took the front seat, next
to the driver. Now he wished he hadn't. Silence was unnatural. It
weighed on them. It wouldn't have mattered so much in the back
seat. There was a kind of invisible barrier between the front and back
seats. Perhaps a survival from the old days, when taxis actually had
a glass partition separating the back from the front.

Quite by chance both men lit cigarettes at the same moment. They
smiled, then got slightly confused deciding who would light whose
cigarette first. A great clumsy show of politeness: finally they lit each
other's cigarette, crosswise.

"Fine lighter you've got there," said the driver.

"It's all right. Had it for years," said the passenger, almost apolo-
getically.

5

"American, eh," said the driver, more as a statement than as a question.

"Not at all. French."

They fell silent again. The taxi crawled on a yard or two. Another car tried to overtake it and squeeze into a better position before turning into Regeneration Avenue. The driver heaved half his body out the window and swore at the other driver, with tremendous energy and relish. After this the two men in the taxi felt more at ease; the silence didn't bother them so much. They smoked quietly, waiting for the lights.

The driver sighed. "Say what you like, this city's no longer fit to drive in."

After a longish pause, the passenger said thoughtfully, "It wasn't a very good idea to make Valdés Street one-way. Now Cabral Street has all the traffic."

"Yes. That's how it is. They try something new, and they only make things worse."

A pause. In a light tone the passenger said, smiling, "Well, they've got to do *something*."

He went on gently, "To justify their existence, you know."

The driver laughed loud. But he cut his laughter short, quite suddenly.

"What do you expect them to do?" he asked angrily. "Only a miracle could solve the traffic problem in this city."

The passenger agreed hastily. "There's absolutely no doubt about it. It's a huge problem. Look at Europe—with all their technical know-how, with all their resources, they still haven't found a way."

They were very near the center now. National Unity Square stretched ahead of them, with its multiple levels, its wide marble steps, its blue cafe-awnings, and the silvery tufts of fountains just beginning to show.

"Do you go abroad often?" asked the driver, in one of those inexplicable transitions from the familiar to the formal "you."

"Once or twice a year. For business, you know."

"I see. What do you do in life? If I'm not being inquisitive."

"Commission broker."

6

Rapid searching glances from the driver.

"And how's business, these days?"

"Fair enough, I suppose."

The driver seemed nonplussed for a moment. Then he slipped into a friendly, confidential tone:

"The furthest I've ever been is Almeida. I've always wanted to travel around a bit, but . . . What's it like, over there?"

"It's all right. It depends . . ."

"Depends on what?"

"I can only speak for Northern Europe, really . . ."

"Germany, eh?"

"England, mostly. I've only been to Germany once."

"England, then. Nice place, eh?"

"I can't say it isn't. Fine cafes and clubs, you know, first-class shops, museums, and the rest of it. But what good is it when it rains every damn day and it's freezing cold. It's got nothing on our climate."

"Yes. True enough. Climate's very important."

There was a formal, reverent pause. They avoided each other's eyes. The passenger lit another cigarette, nervously.

Out of the blue the driver gave a ferocious laugh, something like a bark.

"No place like home, right?"

The other man was silent.

"Even though it's in a bloody mess, eh? Home is home, no matter what, eh?"

The passenger was motionless, speechless. Moved by a sudden impulse, the driver switched on the radio. As the apricot glow of sunset crowned National Unity Square and the first lights came on, brilliant and sad like the first star, the narrow space in the taxi was filled with the loud, brassy sound of a military march. The driver turned up the volume full blast. The air vibrated, the sky flushed purple, and in a tremendous cinemascopic climax, the great neon sign over the square burst into light: the ever-present emblem, the Lion and the Cross.

The passenger said softly:

"Can't you turn it down a bit?"

"What's that?"

The passenger shouted, "Do we have to listen to that disgusting noise?"

The driver laughed again, the same harsh, barklike laugh.

"I see. You don't appreciate music. Very well. As the gentleman wishes."

He fiddled with the knob for a while and stopped at another program. A voice blared out, brassy and loud like the march, an ugly trombone of a voice. The taxi was flooded with it. As if in accompaniment, the fountains on the square were all suddenly lit up at the same time, red, green, blue, the colors exquisitely blending, the splendor complete.

The passenger entrenched himself in silence. He gazed out the window, stubbornly passive. The driver had a fixed, absent-minded smile on his face.

At last the taxi turned into Progress Avenue, leaving behind the fountains, the lights—the power and the glory. Here the evening was unobtrusive, the sunset had already faded. The trees along the pavements shed coolness, a gray tranquillity. There were few shops, and the houses were old.

"Can't you drive faster?" asked the passenger. "There's no traffic here."

The driver leaned over wearily and switched off the radio. He gave a deep sigh. "Are you in such a hurry?" he asked, humbly.

The passenger softened. "I suppose it's just a habit. We're all in a hurry all the time; or we think we're in a hurry."

It seemed to grow darker in the taxi. Perhaps because the dim light from the radio had gone out. The silence was no longer oppressive. It was like a quiet, endless journey, driving through the empty streets of the lower city. The two travelers smoked in silence.

Then the driver spoke again, as if there had never been a break in their conversation:

"Tell me . . . What do they say out there, in Europe?"

"What do they say about what?"

"About us."

A long pause.

"What do you expect them to say," said the passenger softly. "As if you didn't know . . ."

The driver nodded slowly. "I know. Of course I know—who doesn't. What I mean is, hope, is there any hope?"

"There's always hope."

Tired travelers, dark eyes staring straight ahead.

They were nearly there. 33 Santos Street, the passenger had told the driver when he got in—the usual precaution. His real address was 68 Santos Street. It was too late now to give him the right number. So he said nothing. The driver stopped outside the door marked 33.

The passenger opened the door hesitatingly. He put his hand in his pocket, peering at the meter.

"Never mind that," said the driver.

The passenger offered some coins, questioningly.

"I don't want money, I tell you," said the driver crossly.

The passenger got out of the car, still confused. The driver quickly put up his meter-flag, and drove off with a sudden screech of tires. Like thieves, they parted and went their separate ways.

translated by Kay Cicellis

The Actor   TAKIS KOUFOPOULOS

The actor had barely spoken the last word when backstage a me-
chanic pressed the button and the heavy velvet curtain dropped. Now,
to be accurate, the last word was not so much a word as something
like oh or ah or ha or ha-ha-ha. Still, it hardly matters. That's the
way the playwright wanted it, that's how it was in the text, and the
director had agreed: the long monologue—which was really less a
monologue than a series of grimaces and imperceptible movements
on the part of the leading character, with a few words in between,
words such as "here," "there," "afterward," "I'm thirsty," and "you
rats"—anyway, this last monologue was to end with oh or ah or ha
or ha-ha-ha, and the curtain was to drop immediately. In fact, the
director had insisted that the curtain start to fall even before the oh
or ah or ha or ha-ha-ha had been uttered, so as to catch it in midair,
and both should fall together. True, this had caused an argument.
The playwright claimed the curtain would muffle the sound of his
words, which ought to ring out clear and strong. The director said
the thick, heavy curtain would have an even greater impact than the
sound. The playwright insisted—but, since director and playwright
were one and the same person, in the end the actor was instructed
to utter that oh or ah or ha or ha-ha-ha somewhat louder.
So the actor said it loud enough—it rang through the centuries—and

the heavy curtain dropped. What followed is hard to describe; literally, a pandemonium, unique in the annals of such theaters throughout the ages. No Roman arena, no liberation of Paris or successful explosion over Hiroshima, no return of victorious butchers from the various fronts could hold a candle to it. The entire building—that splendid building—was shaken to its foundations as though by a real earthquake. They say the crystal chandeliers were smashed and the walls and ceiling cracked. That may be an exaggeration, but it is a fact that not one of the spectators remained indifferent or unmoved. They were all on their feet, some climbing on the pillars, some standing on the seats, others on the shoulders of the ushers and policemen—who were trembling—as they cheered, whistled, booed, clapped. Even the officials in the first rows—ministers, generals, and so on—took part. They didn't stand up, of course, since everybody knows that the thin little legs dangling from the seats cannot support them any longer. Nor did they clap, for their broad, puffed, heroic chests, covered with names of electoral districts and glorious battlefields, wouldn't allow their hands, hanging from equally thin little arms, to meet. Nevertheless, they shouted at the top of their lungs, "Bravo, bravo—to the gallows, to the gallows!" and waved their short arms and legs.

Even the critics, who had always been unanimously opposed to modern art and had come only to denounce it again the next day from firsthand knowledge, and to put in a formal application for its suppression by the Consul, even they—maybe from fear of the mob's staring, black, round eye, maybe because they thought it wouldn't hurt them after all to keep an open mind about these wild theories (if only those bums who accept them and fall into ecstasy would go and wash a bit, in the same river of blood where they themselves had washed, and then come back for discussion, but on the basis of the eternal principles of art, ethics, and logic and not merely because *he* had said so), or maybe because they had been truly moved by that oh or ah or ha or ha-ha-ha, which was so well timed and so well spoken—anyway, they too put down the crowned busts they were carrying, stuck the actor's head on their lances, raised the lances and waved them. The ladies and young girls, seeing the head on the lances, wagged their fingers at it shouting, "yoo-hoo, yoo-hoo!"

The Actor

Those, however, who had taken the lead in the whole auditorium
were the spectators in the balcony. It was they, really, who had caused
the incident: long before the curtain, before the last act and last cry,
some of them had risen to their feet and begun to analyze and interpret
the play. Their neighbors pulled them by their jackets, the audience
in the orchestra turned and hissed, "Shhhh, shame!" but there was
no stopping them. The director, who was watching through a hole
in the wall, feared they were going to ruin the show. He therefore
gave instructions to the ushers, who rushed up to them and told them
something confidentially (it's rumored those people had been hired
to applaud, and the director threatened to withhold their postpaid
wages, but this is obviously slander)—anyway the ushers told them
something that calmed them down right away. Now these people could
not be controlled. They danced, gesticulated, howled, and then exhorted
the rest of those in the balcony, and they all marched to the railing,
and, one by one, jumped down to the beasts.

Meanwhile, the actor stood motionless behind the curtain, in the
last pose of the play, listening, dazed. He had never dreamed of such
success. Of course he had worked hard for the part, even since childhood. He had sacrificed his whole life, and not only his own. Study,
memorizing, acting, exercises in diction, in impassivity, in pain control,
and above all a program with everything timed neatly—food, sleep,
maxims, all in the proper moment and place. Naturally there had
been no room for weaknesses such as wine, tobacco, or even women—
and not because he was sexless as his enemies asserted. But was all
that enough? Hadn't so many good actors—maybe better ones—almost
failed before him, in that very same play? We say almost, because
some of them did begin by showing a good box office and a number
of beheadings, but in the end it all remained within the circle of the
intelligentsia, it didn't move the masses to hysteria, to genocide, to
folk song, to processions and massacres. To be sure, those others had
not uttered that oh or ah which is so human, and more particularly
that ha-ha-ha which is so divine. The more naive among them pre-
ferred to finish by spitting contemptuously, while the cleverer ones
chose silence. And yet not even that was enough, for ultimately it
is up to the public to decide and the public is imponderable and unpre-

dictable. You never know how to catch an audience: by the hand,
by the collar, or by the neck. Or when to capture it: when it is fasting
or belching, when it is about to murder or has already murdered,
when it is walking into the gas chambers or coming out. You know
nothing about it. Everything is decided on the spur of the moment.
Now the moment looked good.

The actor motioned, people ran to assist him out of his last posture
in the play, he was given something to cover his nakedness, and he
advanced proudly toward the curtain. In the auditorium they were
now chanting his name in three-four time, accompanied by the noise
of the seats and swords. His tiredness was gone, and so were his objec-
tions to the text and the scenery. He no longer worried whether it
was to be Isaac or Iphigeneia, Paul or Saul, "Take aim" or "Fire";
gone too was that fright he had felt in the middle of the performance
when he saw the public yawn, unbutton their waistcoats, and scratch
armpits and cuts—it was then he had turned to the director, trembling,
and the director ordered the auditorium to be sprayed with deodorizer
and the heat turned off. All that was now forgotten. From behind
the curtain came shrieks of applause, firecrackers, wailing. The people
wanted him, they were ready to fall at his feet. History opened the
way for him to sign his name.

The actor reached the middle of the stage, put on his best smile—a
smile of both indulgence and affection—raised the curtain, and stepped
forward. But instead of finding himself in the presence of the worship-
ing public, he encountered a second curtain. It was lucky there was
a double curtain, because as the first one dropped it upset the part
in his hair. He smoothed it down, smiled again, and raised the second
curtain. Only there was a third curtain, then a fourth, a fifth, a
sixth . . . The actor stopped, out of breath. Velvet enclosed him on
all sides. He tried to figure out whether he had walked in the wrong
direction, but no, there he was in the middle, where the two parts
of the curtain meet, the right and the left. He mopped his brow and
thought a while, then suddenly his face lit up. He remembered that
the director had ordered the curtain to be composed of successive layers,
so that the horrible things that happened on stage between acts would
not be heard in the auditorium. The opposite, of course, did not happen,

for everything that took place in the auditorium was audible on stage, but that did not matter. In fact it helped, for it let the director watch the public's reactions and determine how the play was going. Not that he would change the text (even if he wanted to it would have been impossible since the actor—who was a different person—had learned that text and would stick to it), but, depending on the mood of the public, he could alter the sequence of the scenes and so avoid trouble, like the time he presented the Supper scene to an audience that had just finished eating and was therefore totally unmoved.

The actor remembered all that, took heart, and prepared to go on. But suddenly he noticed that the noise from the auditorium decreased, then died down altogether, and in complete silence somebody marched onto the stage and took up a position in the middle, declaring he was a relative of the actor and would now give a funeral oration for him. The actor, who had no relatives, became very angry and began to raise the curtains quickly. But the audience was also annoyed, for, instead of delivering a funeral oration for the actor, the man on the stage was delivering a funeral oration for the audience. Somebody got up and shouted, "What are you talking about?" and two or three others joined him and shouted the same thing, but instead of replying the speaker turned toward them, made the sign of the cross, and the poor fellows instantly melted into thin air. Then the rest became very angry too, stormed the stage, seized the speaker, and set up a summary court of justice to try him for unwarranted exercise of power, and that was the end of him.

It appeared, however, that the man had friends in the audience because, whereas after the incident everybody was ready to resume the applause and lynching, some people—the man's friends, of course—began to say first in whispers, in talk, and finally in bellows that the man was no relative but the actor himself, whom we were waiting for and who had left the stage through a side door, that he used his real face, which we hadn't seen before, and that he had spoken in parables. Naturally, those who set up the court protested, saying this was a lie since the actor had died, and anyone who claimed such things was a heretic. Then the others cried "Traitors," the first group said, "You are instruments of Satan," the second said, "You are instruments of the oligarchy," and since they all had naked swords they rushed at each other. It is hard to record the number of heads that fell and the number of watches and purses stolen. The fighting was mostly face to face—the way the seats were arranged—but often it came to close combat where everyone fired freely, with a number of individual deeds of valor and heroism. The battle had many stages. For a moment one side advanced and the other fell back, then the other advanced and the first retreated, so that it was hard to know whom to bet on. From time to time someone climbed on a seat and shouted, "Brothers!," then both sides quickly stopped, fasted, confessed, turned toward the curtain, lit candles and fire crackers to it, waved swords and amputated arms at it, and then turned back to each other and resumed the butchery.

Meanwhile on the stage the actor was still struggling with the curtain. He went on lifting, one with one hand and one with the other, tensely and hurriedly, for time was running out and the audience—his audience—was slowly forgetting him. True, there remained a few old women and retired officers, but the public, the great public of today and tomorrow, had stopped calling for him after having given him such an ovation. It was busy with other things, with other wars—not his own, and it didn't even mention him in connection with them. It did of course come toward the stage, to light candles and fire-crackers, but this could as well have been meant for the relative. So he had to come out, to appear, to say I am your chosen actor whose name you called out in three-four time. They told you I was dead but I am not dead—because if I were it would be awful for you. I just got entangled in those damned curtains, and other phonies came and took my place and pretended they were me, but here I am now before you, all of me, bring me my speeches so I can see if they are right, bring me my portraits for me to approve, bring your children too so they can contemplate me in my glory and worship me even as you have done. Those were the actor's thoughts as he threw himself wildly against the curtains, opening, raising, pulling, tearing, but there was no end to the curtains.

For a moment in the auditorium one side . . . no, the other . . . or rather—let me have a look—ah, yes, the one side captures the stage.

Then the others, seeing their holy sanctuaries in the hands of the enemy, become very angry, they close ranks, sing their national anthems, increase the portions of mess food, hurl themselves forward, and reach the stage, but then the ones who were watching started shouting, "Dirty bastards!" All right, the others said, and retreated, only to gather fresh momentum and rush forward again, this time not only capturing the stage but routing their opponents. It looked as though the battle was won. Bets were counted, the proper sums for taxes, stamps, and rent deducted, and calculations made as to the amounts due for straight bets, double bets, split bets, and so on. Actually it was not all that simple. For one side, seeing its position was desperate and no help forthcoming from either Saint George of the infantry or the Taxiarchs [patron saints] of the air force, rushed off to get some tough mercenaries and put them in the first lines. As soon as they saw the mercenaries, the other side said, "Oh, yeah?" "Why not!" said the first side. Then the other side rushed and got hold of some of the same mercenaries and the struggle took on new vigor. Fresh incidents, fresh heroes, fresh martyrs, fresh packs of cards and chips, and soon fresh desertions—by those called to the phone or those who lived far away and had to catch the last bus—and again fresh reinforcements and so on and so forth.

In the end, after all of them were slaughtered many times over—it was getting late and we had to go to the office tomorrow—they put on their scarves and overcoats and gradually, chatting in small groups, began to move toward the exit.

After a while the auditorium was empty and quiet. Only a slight rustle could be heard now and then among the curtains.

translated by Rodis Roufos

The Radar SPIROS PLASKOVITIS

Matins were over and the small bell hung silent outside, its tongue
dangling straight down in the windless morning. As he came out of
the chapel, Nikandros threw it a vacant look and instinctively tightened
his cassock round his body. But there was not a breath of wind. Only
the thing that had been creaking for months past could be heard. Today
the sound came more softly, but just as clearly—the thing that had
been nagging day and night like a door ajar in the wind, a door that
refuses either to open or be shut forever. Like Gabriel's soul. All night
long, throughout the last three years, the thing had been creaking
horribly in the darkness and wind . . .

It looked as though the wind had dropped suddenly during matins.
Such a thing is rare at the monastery of Ipsilós which was lashed
by the north-westerlies and the dry, hot southwest winds that whipped
it mercilessly, and the ocean boiled at its feet. "Gabriel must have
quietened down, too," Nikandros thought.

Two hundred meters away, on the rock, the radar now worked without its usual frenzy, turning its steel arms. It creaked normally, it
was bearable—he would have admitted this, if yesterday's goings on
had not surprised him so much. Because yesterday there had been
an awful din. He had not been able to shut an eye right up to the
pealing of the bell. And when the bell rang, he rushed out into the

seething dark, beside himself with the impulse to get away from the sick man's raving in his sleep . . .

"Forgive me!" he shouted to him. "I've forgotten it. Give me your forgiveness, brother. Why don't you forget it, too."

He was lying. That infernal machine never stopped reminding him of it. As soon as he stepped out of the cell he again felt he was lying . . . "No, no, no! You're still waiting, you're still waiting," the radar groaned. "You're always waiting for the Old Man." And there was not a ray of sunlight anywhere, not even that breath of lemon on the mountain.

Covering his ears with his hands, as though he was being stoned, Nikandros finally plunged into the church, while the wind fought to blind him by covering his face with his cassock and grabbing his cap off his head and tossing it away from him.

He went to the burning icon light and crossed himself. Right here was the Abbot's pew, but in bygone days Gabriel had never even leaned against it—except for a tiny bit with his elbow during the all-night Lenten services. For his soul would prop him upright without any support whatever. And at such times his stiff body towered over the pew. Truly, it was hard to believe that the same man could become so small when he prostrated himself later, when he obliterated himself on the flagstones and you could see no sign of him on the floor except for the black cloth. The monks were startled at such passion. In spite of themselves their voices would fade away, expiring in a long-drawn-out murmur. Finally he would sense their presence and raise his head, then unwind and raise his endless body perpendicularly, which now Gabriel could not move from the stool because ankylosis had wrinkled and shriveled it up; but in those days he uncoiled himself smoothly and silently and straight, like a long, warm candle.

"Compared to him I was nothing but a crewman on a caique," Nikandros thought. "He freed me from the caiques, bound me to the rock . . . to the tall, unsinkable brow of the Lord . . ." He remembered the Old Man's first words, when he led him to the monastery as a novice:

"That the ocean may not have power over thee."

"Yes, a caique hand!" and he smiled bitterly. And under his taut

lips felt his unbelievably strong teeth, rooted in their red gums, and
sharp like a wolf's. He put his hand over his mouth to hide them,
as he caught sight of the brothers gathered for matins. Only five or
six of them had remained, sheeplike souls who still dragged behind
them the odor of sleep. If it were not for the bell that summoned them
in the evenings and at dawn, they would scarcely have seen each
other, living as they did among the rows of empty cells and wooden
balconies of the monastery, which had formerly sheltered a host of
monks. But times had changed . . . What was it today that made
people reject the monastic life? And they didn't remember to hold
litanies any more, like the famous one of St. Ignatios, when once a
year Gabriel went down to the town and port to parade the saint's skull.

That's where Nikandros, an innocent young man, had first set eyes
on his form and fell to admiring his bearing. Because this right—the
right to hold the relic on a thick, silken pillow—was enjoyed only
by the Abbot of Ipsilós, where a thousand years earlier Ignatios, Patriarch and defender of the true faith, had become a monk. Even though
he was a prince, Ignatios took orders when he was fifteen years old.
He bound himself to the canon, and castigated the lawlessness of kings
with the law of God. Gabriel knew his passionate writings well. In
those days heavenly matters were not something apart, but the bread
and salt and water of this world here. And just as you kept your
water clean and put the bread in the cupboard lest it get moldy and
make you sick, so people felt in those days that spiritual nourishment
needed protection and daily vigil. Gabriel used to repeat these things
all the time, before he fell prostrate, as he was reading the writings
of Ignatios—saintly Patriarch, whose feast day falls on October 23 . . .

And now? Now there's just these five or six left, the last ones, who
smell of sleep. "Why have they gathered again at matins?" Nikandros
asked himself. What's made them take cover here in these holes so
that the wind tosses them among the ruins like empty pelts. And the
courtyard stinks each morning from the quenched fires of their cooking
pots. Could they have come out of plain stupidity? From some defect
in their bodies? A misdirected life, which from the beginning nested
mistakenly in half-dead bodies, and not knowing where to go, drags
them along and is dragged about by them?"

"But I am hungry and thirsty, Gabriel, and must have the bread
in my hand . . ." That's what he had said. Lies. He had never said
it clearly, his lips had barely uttered it. But Gabriel guessed his vile
thought every time and swore his oath again to him . . . Instead of
getting angry with Nikandros and giving him a canon for repentance
and making him do penitence, instead of binding him to the boards on
his knees till he found himself again, Gabriel smiled strangely and
repeated his oath, in fact he himself reminded him of the oath:

"I shall do what I promised you, Nikandros . . ." And he wanted
him in his cell at night, held Nikandros by the hand, now that he
was bedridden and racked by asthma. "I shall do what I promised
you. By the ninth day of my death, you will see me again . . . By
the ninth day I shall appear to you, and you will have time to repent.
I hear the pulse of your blood," the Old Man whispered. "It's good,"
he whispered softly. "After that you'll have all time before you . . ."
And he made Nikandros' hair stand on end.

The radar groaned outside.

It was summer—last year or the year before—when they set it up.
They'd been forced to spend weeks and weeks breaking rocks before
they could open the road. And what a road! Not even a meter-and-a-
half wide. An army job. They hauled up cement, iron, and wires
on mule-back. They built the guardhouse and brought current up to
it. Then finally, in pieces, packed in large crates, they brought the
new God Baal—that's what Gabriel called it. Baal. In fact he wrote
the name down with his sick hand, because he wanted to complain
to the authorities, to tell them they were committing sacrilege. But
he was no longer the Gabriel whom the Bishop had once stood in mortal
terror of, and who, with his eyes and hands, those huge nervous hands,
forced men in authority to bow their heads before him. Now they
knew he was crippled, and Nikandros had passed outside his cell earlier
and seen his empty cassock hanging from the nail—the Old Man was
exhausted and resting. He never came out to set eyes on Baal.

They threw in more cement and made the antenna firm—two, two-
and-a-half meters high, all meshed steel riveted together, so that the
wind tore itself on it, not finding anything to bite. Then they opened

the boxes. "It's a question of security," they explained. "It listens to the sea . . . It sees through fog and in the dark." The Navy's technicians, the electricians, particularly those in the peaked caps—what an idolatrous nation!—were proud of themselves when they finished their job. Even now, the broken rock, shattered into little pieces and scattered over the mountainside round the monastery, after the engineers' furious efforts to reach the edge of Ipsilós, stood with unfiled edges filed and sharp teeth slashed like razors—for the rain had not had time to wear them down enough to blunt them.

Just two harvests of thistle had managed to shoot up since then. But they blossomed an indigo color. In spring they looked like some noble plantation—maybe tobacco or cotton—which had been left over and had poured over the cliff to merge with the sea below. But the sun withered them quickly, and all the rocky space reappeared in its initial nakedness. You realized once again that it had been hidden only temporarily, that the thistle had become thistle again, and the stone had been hidden by a false green, the scorpion hidden by the stone, and the poison secreted in the scorpion. Today this windlessness still persisted . . .

"Give us your blessing, monk!"

The mocking tone did not escape Nikandros' ear. "Yes, bless us," they said from the guardhouse. He turned and saw them, saw him. Bending almost doubled over the small cement terrace was the new petty officer. He'd hung his bovine head over the ledge; his hair was tousled, and health brimmed from his open undershirt. A barbarous health, immoral, Nikandros thought.

"I don't know you," he replied. "When did they take the others away?"

"Three days ago," the petty officer said. He was a bit more reserved now, apparently a bit startled by the monk's appearance. "Nice place to stay."

"I've been here thirty years, young man; the Abbot twice that."

"You can keep it! We weren't drafted to become monks. 'The Navy' they called it. Okay then, 'Navy!' Now you try and tell me what kind of navy this is. Just because they put up this pile of old junk here . . ."

Spiros Plaskovitis

He scratched his neck with his left hand, tapping a metal cup with
his right. His tunic was thrown over his shoulder casually, so that
the sleeves with their two stripes dangled.

"The way things are going, we'll spend the whole winter here.
Which means we're going to see our livers through," the petty officer
grumbled, working himself up into a state. "And to cap it all we'll
lose our girl friends." His tongue stuck over the word "girl." "Why,
it's as if they'd taken our girls away from us . . ."

Nikandros begain to shift away, but the young man stuck his head
out even further over the ledge. He clinked the cup again.

"Dice!" he called. "Don't you play, monk? Scared?"

"Who should I be scared of?" Nikandros mused, looking around
him. "Only the eye of God . . ." At that hour the sun fell full on
the guardhouse. Just a few paces further on, the open arms of Baal
shaved the thistles with their shadow. "It listens to the sea, sees through
fog and in the dark," he repeated to himself.

"Have you ever played dice?"

"I'm an old caique hand," he answered.

"Prove it . . ."

Half a minute later he was among them, having strode up the three
cement steps. Apart from the petty officer, the others were no better
than startled riffraff. They blinked, as though the cassock had tossed
soot in their eyes, and they dug their hands in their pockets. They
had been there long enough to plaster the walls with pictures of naked
girls clipped from magazines and newspapers, and now they were
trying to cover them up with their backs.

"Let's spread the blanket out."

"The money first," Nikandros said.

They froze. "The money first . . ." The words leapt like a razor
from an old sheath. The sheath had grown moldy, uncared-for and
forgotten, but the razor was as keen as it ever was. He was dazzled
now that he saw it again, now that he heard it again. Thirty years
it had been growing moldy, and there it was again! "The money first!"
Surely they were already dead scared of his throw—the scoundrels!—
scared of the way he could juggle the little black-spotted cubes in
his hand, and then spin them furiously down on the blanket.

24

At their age he used to shout it out on purpose, hammering it home,
right in everyone's face: "The money first!" But it wasn't
what he had had in mind. He just wanted things on the level. He
wanted to see clearly what he was playing for, what he was winning—
otherwise he didn't enjoy the game. And he didn't want to be cheated
either. So all this, whether he liked it or not, had boiled up in him,
made his palm itch. In the harbor he had had his own caique, and
a two-storied house left him by his grandfather. Gabriel used to tell
him how he'd met that middle-aged man with his almond-shaped mocking eyes, in the years of Turkish rule, his portrait forgotten on one
of the walls of the house for his grandson, who was still a child, to
gape at. The low fez, his short fur jacket and waistcoat adorned with
gold cord and small buttons. It seems that once the tinkle of his money-
pouch touched the ears of the Sultan Hamit, who thereupon decided
to invite him to his table. He decorated him with a weighty medal,
and in order to see him wear it more stiffly, added a poisoned cake
to the treat. So, grandfather returned with the star on his fur coat,
which they even pinned to his portrait. As for him, they put him
in the graveyard.

It was autumn. He and two others sat cross-legged in the bows of
his caique like three big crabs, leaning their backs against the quay,
throwing dice. And once again his eyes, his breath, chased after the
leaping cubes. His yearning to master them, to teach them where to
stop, which side up to show, warmed them in his hands. There was
a breeze coming from the sea, and the anchor-rope was creaking—
something like the tremolo a cicada makes in summer. The breeze
tried to pull everything in, toward the stores along the quay. Inevitably
they saw it snatch their money. They had it under a roof-tile between
their legs, but someone accidentally kicked the tile and the filthy bills
rose in a whirlwind and scattered round the harbor. The men were
up and after them, and the bills then fell among the people, the priests.
Totally absorbed in their game, they had neither seen nor sensed a
thing. At that very moment the skull of Saint Ignatios was going past,
in the hands of Gabriel, whose memory is celebrated October 23 . . .

The following afternoon the abbot again appeared before the moored
boat, but not like yesterday when he'd been in his full liturgical vest-

ments. Now he was unadorned, all in black. He strode into the bows as though he had been blown there, and came and stood next to Nikandros. He'd come on purpose, certain he'd find him there alone. But who could possibly have let him know? He tapped the sailor gently on the shoulder.

"Have you any ouzo?" he asked.

Nikandros was aghast. He dived hurriedly down the trap-door into the hold and brought out a flask, then rummaged around for the small raki glasses. But Gabriel said, "Don't bother," and brought the flask to his mouth. The dusky hour was spreading over the sea.

"We all need something strong. Yet alcohol is weaker than a mother's milk." He folded his cassock round him and settled down on the planks of the deck. "Milk," he went on to himself, "builds bones. It props the infant up on its legs in a few months. You know I can remember you since then. Since the time I gave your mother extreme unction. She'd had Spanish flu. You were stumbling around the room, trying to latch on to her body somehow . . ."

Still staring at the sea, he fell silent. The sailor grabbed the flask and shook it; it seemed empty. He tried to drink from it; it was empty. He kicked it away.

"But who remembers milk, our first source of strength, eh?" The abbot asked.

"It's finished . . ." the sailor mumbled and kicked the flask further away.

The abbot stretched. As he spread his arms out, they appeared unnaturally big, they reached into the sky where they began to darken the clouds. Then suddenly, for one endless minute, he looked into Nikandros' eyes.

"What shall it profit you if you gain the whole world and lose your soul?" he asked.

"Mercy, monk, you've ruined us!" the petty officer growled, pulling back. He'd worked himself up into a temper.

"Man, these are the devil's own dice. Where did we dig him up, man?" one of the louts muttered under his breath.

"That's one month's wages gone," the short one with the kiss-curl whimpered to himself.

They all began to moan and groan. "You, a man of God, taking our money."

"And what possessed you to play with a man of God?"

Nikandros raked up the last coins from the blanket, tied them in his handkerchief, and tucked the handkerchief under his cassock. Just then somebody pushed the other door of the guardhouse open. The radar machinery came partly into view: metal boxes and wires and electric bulbs, and in the midst of all these, a milky, illuminated square. Millions of spots seemed to be dancing crazily in its light. They raced toward the center of the square, making strange, small whistling sounds, then were lost in its depths.

"So that's how it works, eh?" he asked the petty officer for want of something better to say.

"Night and day, without stop . . ." the other replied morosely.

"Night and day . . . And how will you know when something's up?"

"You mean if it catches what we're afraid it might catch? Don't worry, they've got all that fixed up. The alarm goes off by itself. Come on now . . ." and he winked, "give us back half of it at least. What will you do with it? My girl might be arriving any day now, you understand?" While he was speaking, agitated as he was, he struggled to get his arms into the sleeves of his tunic, but without success.

"I've become what I was once," Nikandros thought. "I've played dice. I've won. If only Gabriel could see me! Seventy-two years on the rock of Ipsilós just to save his soul and mine—he promised me that . . . But how does he know I trusted him? What did his mind apprehend that I haven't been able to see yet? Small, mad dots in infinity."

He chuckled, and with the bovine gaze of the young man following him, descended the steps heavily.

"Well, there's nothing to be done, my dear chap. Each according to his luck," he said quietly.

"You dirty monk . . . You dirty monk . . ." the petty officer swore after him.

Gabriel got up and went over to sit on his stool. He didn't realize what he had done until he actually felt himself sitting down. It was something that happened to him very rarely of late; a sudden power, a wind drove him from the mattress, the same force that had deprived his sick body of the little weight that remained to it. And all of a sudden he would find himself in the middle of the cell, as though in some new place, and he would see larger and livelier icons around him.

"Might be a sign that I'm going to die today," he thought happily. He inspected his brown inner cassock and black slippers, then crossed himself, sighed, and rang the little bell to summon the others.

"Holy father!" the novice exclaimed when he pushed the door open. "The Almighty has restored you . . ."

Gabriel told him to fill the holy lamps with oil and asked for a pinch of incense to smell.

"Death is our health, my child," he whispered. "Inform the brothers that the Abbot is bidding them farewell today. But not quite yet. Later I shall summon them all here. For the moment just go and call Nikandros. I cannot hear the wind, or the other . . . Baal . . ." he whispered, his voice dropping even lower. "What's happening?"

"The day is calm, holy father. There's not a leaf stirring outside."

"Nothingness is a sign of God. The world is hubbub and movement and revelation, my child. But God expresses Himself in Nothing. For no man shall see His face and live . . ."

The novice kissed his hand and left.

"Yes," Gabriel assured himself. "Today I shall die." He felt impatient and at the same time new, like a bridegroom. "Praise be to Thee, Lord, praise be to Thee! This ennui, this pang of days—at last. But I must not hurry . . . Hey, brother Nikandros, where are you?" He shored himself up on his feet. "Well, well, I'm standing," he said. "Brother Nikandros, I'm standing, do you see? Without any effort. I am absolutely light. I have pleasant news to tell you. I feel it in advance. This lightness means I can go and return . . ."

But just as the door was opened, as though he had been given a shove, the Abbot collapsed on his stool.

"Nikandros, you've got a lot of mud on your shoes," he frowned. Then he cried weakly, "Who are you then to claim the price of your doubt, who think you must live again in order to die a just man?"

"I have not asked for anything, Old Man. Only your forgiveness," Nikandros said, prostrating himself and embracing the Abbot's knees in supplication. There was silence as Gabriel laid his hands on the bowed head.

"And yet, and yet . . . When you followed me, I took that oath upon my head. I have not forgotten it, and you have not forgotten it, no. If you had forgotten, I would have seen it. My conscience has tormented my day. 'And how do I know,' you said, 'that I'll save my soul?' You were a young man near the sea. Why should you not try your luck? All the creatures of the earth gamble. Their loss is another's gain . . ."

The same old story, Nikandros thought.

"You forced me to take the oath because I loved you. I had already completed the fourth indhiktion* of my monastic life. It was exactly at the time that it was obvious you had not forgotten . . ."

"Forgive me . . . Forgive me . . ." Nikandros whispered again.

But the Abbot was holding his head down firmly with his hand, and would not allow him to struggle. It was as if he was nailing him down on that old incident, on that drunken conversation that had escaped from Nikandros one evening.

. . . He'd gone down the mountain with the donkey, down to the fishing village of Sangri for the monastery supplies, and the grocer there had plied him with ouzo. He had seen the sea close by once again, and the caiques moored round the old Genovese fortress. The grocer had lowered the blinds because the afternoon sun was blinding. "Here's health to you, monk," he had said after the fourth glass. "Monk?" Nikandros asked in alarm. He looked at his hands, his clothes, and wondered. "Monk!" he kept on whispering all the way back with the loaded beast. Blind drunk, he labored up the hill. "Monk . . . He's right . . . Monk!" And in the evening, when he was sitting next to the Abbot and burning inside like a charcoal brazier, he burst into loud guffaws when Gabriel said:

"It's the sixtieth year I've been in this cell, Nikandros."

* An ecclesiastical term meaning a cycle of fifteen years.

"Just imagine," he responded, "if you've goofed, and we've all fooled ourselves too . . . Just imagine if there's nothing beyond . . ."

Gabriel did not speak immediately. He just lifted the edge of his cassock and covered his face, then he spent the whole night praying. For the first time he tied himself with steel rope to the hooks in the storehouse, and stayed there for three days and three nights. On the fourth day he summoned him to his Abbot's quarters.

"I have received permission," he said gravely. "You will get your proof. I swear it to you. I have received permission to return to thee from the other world. In our holy Byzantium, communication took place frequently."

The years passed, the Old Man's years stretched on too far.

"My conscience tormented me," he repeated. A terrible thought crossed Nikandros' mind just then: "He always knew how to kindle my impatience. That was his art! Day and night he would keep me on tenterhooks. Night and day, just like the arms of the radar . . . Why do you care about me any more?" he felt like shouting. "You've settled accounts with this world with your sacrifice, so why should anything that happens now matter to you?"

But he said nothing, seeing Gabriel's advanced state of feebleness. Before nightfall, in truth, the Abbot had become as light as a twig. Two or three times Nikandros carried him to his bed then brought him back to the stool, all with the greatest ease. Each time he managed to summon enough strength he spoke to the monks, and they, down on their knees or prostrate before him, filled the little room with their black backs and woolen caps. Then Nikandros heard him mixing up accounts of incidents from the days of Sultan Hamid, as he advised and blessed him. Nikandros could not quite make out whether the old man was praising the infidel or censuring him.

"The enemy gives us our glory and our victory," he whispered in a strange voice. "That is why the Lord said love your enemies. What kind of glory would man have without victory? And how can he be victorious without enemies? But you must not accept the medals and honors they heap upon you. Love your enemy, my brothers, but do not repose yourselves beside him. He could at that moment put you

to death. Which is what happened to the grandad of our brother
Nikandros . . .''

He looked at him with a sweet smile. "Light your candles," he said
suddenly, "I am bidding you farewell."

Gabriel's death stunned the neighboring villages. The news traveled
quickly to the town as well, where, in their memories, the older folk
still preserved the picture of the man as they had known him in their
youth. His great age alone was sufficient to promote him to sainthood,
aside from the fact that his soul was unsullied.

The very next morning, crowds of peasant women, a number of
old fishermen, all in the company of two or three priests and a shepherd
still leading his ewe, began the trek up to the monastery to pay their
respects to the Abbot's remains. But in the afternoon, and on the morning of the second day, a host of folk arrived, many from farther
away. They settled as best as they could in the empty cells of the
monastery, waiting for the funeral, and piously attending the continual
prayers in the church round the dead Abbot, who sat propped up
on his throne, looking just as he had in his days of glory years before,
dressed in his vestments and the insignia of his rank, with his fingers
shaped in the sign of benediction, while the incense hovered near him
in a bluish fog.

After the calm that had lasted a day and a night, the wind began
to batter Ipsilós. It fell with its back against the rock, having first
scraped the ocean a little toward the north, where a small, fluffy cloud
appeared to be sitting. At that point the sea became curly, the water
turned grayish blue, then foam burst forth, as though under the impact
of some great tumult. The wind struck people on the road, spurred
them on, hitting them hard and ruffling their clothes and blankets.
And while they slept that night, it battered the walls of the monastery,
like some old siege-engine.

This entanglement of wind and death made its mark on everybody's
face on the second day, because everyone now had to keep opening
and closing his eyes and nostrils, and stammer rather than speak, like
a person choking in the smoke of a fire. Something inexplicably stinging

was in the air. And as they left each liturgy, where Gabriel's skeletal sign of benediction hung like a beak above their heads, they struggled to distinguish the flight of birds from the radar.

"You smell sweet. Your whole body smells sweet," he said, bending very low over her neck. "It was nice of you to come."

The girl was silent, sighed gently.

"Aren't you scared?" she whispered. "I've never seen anything like it before. He looks as though he's alive . . . Do you see his hand? That hand of his there, the way he's holding it up? Lord forgive me!" and she crossed herself.

"They must have him tied," he answered. "I'm sure he's being propped up somehow from underneath. You know what monks are."

"Tied! You think so?" and she shoved him away gently with her back. Her body was all restless. He had been touching her impatiently from the moment they came in. The woolen material of his tunic had a warm roughness, the roughness of a young soldier. It made her skin tingle, and the down on her arms stood on end in the yellow candle light.

"Not so close . . ." she begged even more quietly. "They'll see us."

He threw a quick glance around, bent down, and whispered in her ear, "That's how I like it. Leave me alone. I know what I'm doing." Then: I like it," resting his hand on her waist just above her hip. The hip tensed briefly, then relaxed, carrying the vibrations of her belly right up to his arms.

"They say he became a saint even while he was still alive," she said, awestruck. He cleared his throat.

"Huh . . . Things like that only happened in the old days. They don't make saints nowadays."

"He'll be the last one. My aunts told me. I really don't know."

"Where did you leave the old crones?"

"I gave them the slip to come and find you."

"But . . . you're my fiancée aren't you? So, you do whatever you want."

"Are they going to bury him in a sitting position, as they do with Bishops?" the girl changed the subject once more.

Now he was pressing against her shamelessly. He'd wriggled his hand into her loose blouse, having first undone the snaps, and was now busy feeling her armpit.

"What do you mean? . . . You mean without a coffin?"

"Come on now, stop it. You're just making fun . . ."

"Will they plant him in the earth just as he is? Huh . . . Huh . . ." His breath came in grunts. "Just think, what would I have done if you hadn't come? I'd have been sick. I tell you I really would have been sick. Your tit's grown a bit," he said, his voice muffled in her hair.

"Let's get out, I'm scared . . ."

"I like it, next to the dead body like this, and the incense. I like it, d'you hear?"

"Ah! You're going to damn my soul. Let's get out . . ."

He chased her. They chased each other in the darkness outside, their eyes still blinded by the candlelight in the church. The wind had raised the dust and a stench came from the ruined buildings. As they stumbled on piles of animal dung, choked at the pungent smell, and paused as sudden pain peppered their eyes.

"What have I done to you to make you drag me about like this?"

They clasped hands tightly. His fingers crushed hers, and her nails pierced his palms. They pushed and pulled at each other, never letting go.

"What have I done to you?" she asked desperately. "It's terrible here, it smells . . ."

"I like it," the petty officer said. "It's nice that it's terrible." And he pulled her on top of him.

Gabriel's funeral was held on Sunday morning, and before it was even noon his sacred remains were lost forever to this world. The church was now empty, but it had had no time to go cold and revert to its customary gloom. It still preserved something of the warmth of the candles and the breath of the multitudes that had congregated, like the hide of a newly slaughtered beast that still keeps part of the warmth of the detached flesh.

Nikandros closed the double doors. "The time limit's starting," he thought in spite of himself, and looked up. He crossed the courtyard and made for his cell. It was the first time in three days he had heard the radar. "And yet it's been blowing all this time and that things's been working all this time . . ." he thought. But with all the vigils and the almost total fast, he'd reached a stage of deafness and he couldn't see properly either. He was whispering chants for the Abbot's soul and sensed the people around him and their genuflections—a vision of bygone ages, the times when everyone helped you to attain canonization, the times when saints or visionaries were more common than blind beggars. Now the monastery was returning to its desolation. Tonight, tomorrow at the latest, the last pilgrims would be going back to their villages, and already the inebriation of faith, which Gabriel had inspired with his death, was dying out.

"I need a good night's sleep," Nikandros said to himself. "I have to be in good physical shape to face the next few days. But . . . what's a physical shape anyway?"

While he was taking his cassock off in his cell, he suddenly realized he was afraid to sleep. For a long time he stood wavering above the bedclothes. Gabriel could only appear to him in his sleep, at which point the game would be played for keeps . . .

In utter exhaustion he sat at the edge of the bed, near the bedpost. He spread his hands out on the blanket, and its woolly down seemed to crawl into his flesh. Then it climbed up his shoulder poured over his spine, and was sucked into his entire body as he sucked it in . . . down that was alive, a dull voiceless call to his tired bones that had almost pierced his knees through standing motionless for so long. He shook himself "No, I must not sleep," he said. "No!"

He went out and poured a cup of water over his head, then came back and put some coffee on. He dug up an old newspaper and, swallowing the coffee gulp by gulp, began reading. The small leaden letters soon started leaping from the page, whirling in the air, and disappearing in some invisible distance, just like the spots on the radar. For a few minutes he managed to repeat the phrases over again in a loud voice, but then got tied up and fell into a mumble so that he couldn't make out what he was saying. Finally, he shoved the coffee cup away, and for a fleeting moment had time to see the dregs—a long black stain spilling into the saucer.

This time he slept. For how long? Perhaps as long as it takes to recover from a faint or make a deep prostration. There were monks who, during the all-night services of Easter Week, dropped off while they were on their knees, and then you had to pick them up from the floor and shake them awake. A yellow light now dripped from the skylight as the afternoon retreated, but the pane clattered, clattered. The wind would not leave it in peace. Fear hammered in his chest. This was no waking up, it was a brutal sundering, a punch from within that had knocked him over.

"What am I doing?" he asked himself. "Sleeping."

He tried to work out how long it had been. The coffee stain in the saucer was completely dry. "Yet the old man hasn't come yet," he thought with relief. "Which means I could have gone on sleeping. "But then a second voice spoke up within him. "You don't know about that. You don't know about that." He threw the cassock over himself, stuck a nail into his belt and left the cell. It was getting dark.

He managed it. By a great painful effort, he managed to stay awake that night and the following morning. Every time sleep weighed like lead on his eyelids, he reacted by punching at his belt. The nail entered his flesh and the pain forced his eyes open again. But his great fear was lest he fall asleep with his eyes open, for he had heard that could happen too. When all the other monks had settled down, the hours dragged on unbearably. He could find nothing to do apart from sweeping the empty space around him with the same terrible rhythm of the radar. His concentration gave the machine fantastic dimensions. He felt it spreading its roots deeper and deeper into the rock of Ipsilós, and its charged soul tossed its magnetic waves to the furthest limits of the dark landscape. Then it received them back again and again and again . . . "For ever and ever amen," he mumbled absently, staring at the red lights of the antenna from the balcony.

But he couldn't stand it any more. As he was returning from the wooden balcony he tripped on the wooden threshold of the cell, and felt a terrible dizziness. He dragged himself on for two or three steps and fell prostrate on the bed with his arms spread out. That's when Gabriel came.

Perhaps it was dawn breaking. First he saw the earth opening up like a yellow cloud. Something that looked like earth and steam, but which was neither on the earth nor in the sky. From there the Abbot's hands rose—two bony rods emerging from the wide sleeves of his cassock. Then, without his stove-pipe hat on his head, his lean face appeared, bathed in perspiration, as though it were made of wax. His thin hair and straggly beard hung wet and matted. And before he could sink back into his earthy cloud he managed to shout out to him twice: "Nothing! Nothing!"

Nikandros moaned and fell back on the mattress.

"You were had, and you fooled me too . . . You were had and you fooled me too . . ." he repeated incoherently. "Didn't I say it would be like that, Old Man?"

He hurled a host of questions about their past life, and also accusations against Gabriel. He prowled up and down his cell and cursed his bed. Finally, he pulled his trunk out feverishly and began rummaging through it. He paused midway, got up and bolted the door. Then he went to each wall and turned the icons round, then back to his trunk from which he pulled out a cotton shirt and an old jacket.

"I'll take the scissors with me. I'll do the rest on the way. I'll leave the cassock and cap there . . . And my beard too . . ." he muttered laughing crazily.

He opened the door to see what was going on outside. Nobody! Just that ceaseless grinding of the mill-like radar. He waited a while and closed the window again without moving from where he was. The light of day stuck to the panes.

"Yet he appeared to me!" he whispered.

translated by N. C. Germanakos

Going Home   ALEXANDROS KOTZIAS

The locomotive pumped thick black smoke over the outlying slums, whistling once or twice as though relieved at having left their stifling misery behind and come up onto the great rise; the cars rocked obediently, then turned and rolled like a string of beads into a poplar wood, hidden. A moment later all Salonika was gone.

Petros Papaloukas turned away from the open window. He tossed his black beret onto his suitcase in the netting overhead, and sat down, his broad, powerful back erect but relaxed, not needing to rest against the seat. He loosened his khaki tie and unbuttoned his collar. Oof! Heat, sweat, his shirt stuck to his skin. The sun was still up. But he finally had the discharge papers in his shirt pocket. Early that morning in Kozani he said goodbye to the tank corps, turned in his government equipment, and with two signatures and an official seal he was no longer a lieutenant. Four years . . . he was a civilian again, free at last. Tomorrow home.

"Just twelve hours and we'll be there!" Tsangarakis leaned into the compartment from the narrow corridor, his big buck teeth flashing an ingratiating grin. "Nothing worth looking at in first class. How about a stroll to third?"

Petros shook his head no.

"They're playing backgammon. Want to watch? It's fun."

"No."

"God, what a furnace! Want a soda? They're cold. Want me to get you one?"

"No."

"Brrr! What a warm welcome!"

Tsangarakis tripped, probably on purpose, over a fierce-looking major who was reading the *Chatter* and muttering syllables from under his walrus moustache. He sprawled on an empty seat near Petros, looked reflectively at his fingernails, uncut and black as mourning, and rubbed his bony fingers briskly together. Then, softly whistling a waltz, he spotted two lieutenants, one blond, one brown haired, both with trim moustaches, sitting on the seat opposite. They were silent and motionless, as if painted on the wall. Soon he lost interest in that game too, sat up, yawned, and slapped himself on the back of the neck, knocking his hat down to a rakish angle over his right eyebrow.

"Hey, hey, buddy, by tomorrow night we'll be strolling around little Old Falieron." He linked his arm through Petros'. "Kid, did your ship go down? Why the long face? You poor bastard, we'll be in Athens demain matin."

Petros Papaloukas withdrew his arm as if to look out the window. Damn Tsangarakis! Buddies with that pimp? And what was his first name? In basic training at Haidari they'd done two months in the same company . . . and yes, long ago, second or third year in high school, boy scouts in the same troop. What rotten luck! At noon, when the bus from Kozani stopped at Gida for two minutes, former Lieutenant Tsangarakis had squeezed in, carrying an old split suitcase tied together with cord. From then on he appointed himself Petros' intimate friend and protector, recounted his erotic adventures to him at length, touched him for all his small change, and tried to sell him a wonder-working sexual stimulant. He stuck to him like a suction-cup and bled him.

And now the entire plain was opening up, wide, immense. Puffs of smoke left behind by the train in the burning airlessness hung here and there like small brown cotton clouds marooned in the dazzling blue. Orchards, vegetable gardens, telephone poles chasing each other out of sight, shacks, bushes, solitary churches, telephone poles, harvested fields, shacks, telephone poles . . . I'm twenty-five years old, Petros thought, twenty-five and a half. The problem must be resolved now, it can't wait any longer, things have blown up at home. He pressed his lips together stubbornly. He's gone too far, he's ruined mother's health with his ways and his whore. Mother had an attack and collapsed, her face turned blue, cardiogram, medicines, doctors, she's short of breath, can't breathe, and he laughs at her and tells her to stop acting. That wise, decent, proper man—imagine! What a transformation!

Tsangarakis ground out his cigarette with his heel. "Bo-oof!" he grunted, at loose ends and looking for someone or something to harpoon. "No offense meant, Lieutenant . . . May I?"

"Of course!" the darker lieutenant groaned, as a wrinkle dug into his low forehead.

"I feel like talking, you know? I warble freely like a bird, if you don't mind. And besides, with your permission, Lieutenant, I'm an orphan and have to make myself agreeable. That is, practically an orphan, since my mama and papa, bless them, are in perfect health."

The dark lieutenant frowned, but a smile broke out on the lips of the blond lieutenant. Tsangarakis turned smoothly to his new audience. He waved his arms, grimacing dramatically.

"And what good are they to me alive, Lieutenant? A man is nowhere in the modern world without social connections, right? Now my friend over here, this guy is a wheel, a boy wonder, Lieutenant—what's eating him?" He winked slyly. "But what am I? A naked snail with two greedy old parents, vampires, for me to feed and wipe their asses. And what have they given me but their blessing? God, if the Minister of Public Order hadn't taken me under his wing I'd have become a priest. Don't laugh, Lieutenant. In this dog's life everyone needs a wing to shelter under. Even you, pardon me, Lieutenant . . . that is . . . if you don't have the cash get a surplice or a sash!" He tapped him twice on the knee. What a fool, what crap! Petros thought, and kept staring out the window.

A threshing machine next to a ruined stone wall cast a white cloud over the insectlike farmers dragging it around. They dropped behind, far back, out of sight, and again fields, orchards, telephone poles. Well, so the war is finally over . . . Peace everywhere . . . Ten years of war, slaughter, devastation, occupation, revolution, a second revolution, ten years in all. Father began it in Albania. I was a child then. Now the people are working, they work hard, they sweat, but they don't get killed. The telephone poles passing by are whole, but then they were all down, they blew them up with dynamite and mines, mines, every step an ambush, not a bridge left standing, thank God the war's been over for nearly two years. And since morning he was through with the army, and most important he wasn't seriously hurt—only five teeth lost—Petros fingered the deep scar on his lower right cheek.

Tsangarakis now swelled like a stunted turkey. He was still talking, flying high, his tongue racing like a greased pig. "I'm wildly happy today, no offense, Lieutenant, it's my nature, as they say I'm a poet, a versifier of life condemned by necessity to wear myself out in business matters. In place of a soul the Almighty planted a neat little tune in me, say a foxtrot. Only He made me a bit nearsighted and damn it I didn't see that monstrous jeep so I didn't salute, I kept my hands in my pockets, watching a skirt. A catastrophe, Lieutenant. Burned! Scalded! for not saluting a jeep."

"A jeep?" The blond lieutenant suppressed a laugh.

"Fate, Lieutenant, a green jeep. Because the jeep slams on its brakes in front of me and out leans the third-in-command of the army, a great big beast of a general, he curses me back and forth and hallelujah it's the ascension of Tsangarakis, blown to Division 525 the very same day. 'You mole, you blind mole!' says Jimmie the minister. 'What do you expect me to do? When it comes to that dragon I wash my hands, he's got it in for you. Get over there and get your discharge in the beautiful outdoors; you're going on a picnic.' That's right, Jimmie, a little picnic just three weeks long. But to eat the whole donkey, if you'll pardon the expression, and just as you're finishing up the tail, like that! for a jeep. And bye-bye to my schemes. This little picnic loused me up in a terrific deal, Lieutenant, at least a half roll of pounds sterling flew out of my hand. And that, begging your pardon, is why I'm wildly happy. Athens, Athens! For you the birds are singing—the flowers are springing . . ."

"I don't understand, you said that you were employed while in the service?" the dark lieutenant said acidly.

"I am constantly employed, Lieutenant. I labor night and day. It's tough on a guy who's an orphan twice over."

"And what do you do?"

Tsangarakis, very pleased with himself, exploded in a sudden laugh. "Greek industry, Lieutenant, Greek industry. Get the point?"

"No."

"I run a little office, I arrange what I can. Your humble and eager servant in whatever you require."

"Bah! What kind of work?"

"All kinds, for everyone, Lieutenant. Here's my office." He struck his forehead and leapt to his feet. "Little heartbeat, where have you been all my life?" he whinnied.

A plump, bow-legged girl with cheeks like peaches was swaying down the aisle. Tsangarakis tripped again over the major's laced boot and slid to her feet.

"Sweetheart . . . wh-whew! Je viens!"

Petros sighed with relief . . . A herd of goats was running toward the river. The train slowed, screeching suddenly, and scattered the goats, and a barefoot shepherd was shooing them away, thin, sun-blackened, mummylike. The bridge's iron girders groaned with a deep anguished vibration and the steel mass rolled slowly, carefully, as though balancing over a chasm. The river was an expanse of white boulders, their nakedness flashing vengefully in the savage light. Petros frowned. Then again the safety of meadows, land, the temporary safety. The rhythmic vibration faster, faster, unchecked: rock white rock whiterock whiterockwhite . . . cardiogram and he says you're pretending, he who once would have given his life for us all. He couldn't care less when I was wounded, as though he never knew me. Yet once his smile was warmer than a friend's. At Haidari the last night, when they shipped us off to Reserve Officers' School, he stood outside the gate in the midnight sleet in February, exhausted, soaking wet, just to see me off, and as I leaned out of the truck, his stiff hand grasped mine: "So long!" The truck rolled downhill, night swallowed us, and he was still standing in a beret, a scarf, and a

long dark coat, under the lantern at the gate with the sleet lashing
his face. He waved his hand as though reaching to touch me and
was left behind, gone, the smile gone. At the convention in Florence
a few days afterward he met that whore and came back a different
man, when I was wounded . . . the whole mountainside burning like
hell, when the mine threw up an earthquake of black smoke. The
armored car went up like a haystack. How did I jump out of the
flames, tumble behind mastic trees? Antonakis fired at me, I was quick
enough to plant one right between his eyes before he fired another
round, I took care of him, but Takis the Joker was wedged at the
controls howling, the column in flames, fire and iron, thirty-five
ambulances, ambush outside of Aspraggeloi, we were bringing the
wounded down from Grammos to Yannina, the sky black from burning
gasoline, clouds of it over the savage light, what a blaze! Stench of
burning from the wounded, from Takis the Joker. And later Antonakis
beside me in the calm; hours and hours beside me until they picked
me up, motionless on my back in the low branches under the open
sky, the merciless sun, and he dead beside me. Glassy eyes like beads,
body shrunken like a mummy. Was he seventeen years old? Petros
shifted uneasily. And why did I name him Antonakis? Maybe he
was Mitros or Kotsos or Panagyi, so many, many guerrillas were
shepherd boys.

The train slowed again as more little houses began to appear among
the orchards. The village cemetery with whitewashed walls and under
its scattered cypresses a priest in high hat and vestments, and a woman
in black, on her knees burning incense over a gravestone . . . At last
the train came to a stop. There was no one in the bleak station, only
rusty sheet iron, cow dung, and a bad smell. A short distance beyond
the platform was a green two-story house, and a fat, overdressed,
painted woman watched the tracks from the window, chewing gum,
waiting. Behind her on the wall of the room a shawl, a string of garlic,
a mirror. Waiting for what? In the neighboring yard a donkey stood
utterly still and mindless in the burning sunlight. An emaciated old
woman wearing a dark blue slip squatted, chewing seeds in the shade
of a fig tree; she too watched the tracks, her toothless mouth grinding
hungrily, constantly spitting out seeds. Waiting for what? As the sun

hammered down it seemed as if nothing were moving on the sizzling earth, and the flaming air was absolutely silent, motionless, unbreathing, as if the vengeful merciless light suddenly turned black. Petros closed his eyes.

When he reopened them the train was moving again. The fat woman in the window was still chewing gum, the green house was gone.

Just then a thundering voice filled the corridor. "That's not the proper uniform for an officer." In the aisle was the corner of a huge suitcase, and the voice boomed in like a church bell. "As long as you're in uniform you are not a civilian, sir! Shut up! I'll have you court-martialed!" The suitcase entered. Lifting it was a tall, fat colonel with rosy, puffed cheeks, whose outburst left him panting. Behind him Tsangarakis holding a big basket suffered the dressing-down like a Magdalen. In fact his dirty, wrinkled uniform, with pockets split at the seams, was a dishrag.

The officers in the compartment rose. From the corner of their eyes the two lieutenants watched Tsangarakis with satisfaction, the brown-haired one perhaps with malice. Petros buttoned his collar, tightened his tie. Tsangarakis struggled to get the basket and suitcase into the netting, then crumpled like a withered leaf next to Petros.

The colonel was still breathing heavily, wheezing, from time to time pulling out an endless plaid handkerchief, like a tablecloth from a cheap restaurant, and mopping his perspiration. Settled in the seat opposite he fixed his small bloodshot eyes intently on Petros' chest, on the two small multicolored ribbons.

"You must be a regular officer, Lieutenant," he said abruptly at last. But his conviction at once gave way to astonishment. Then he was discharged today! With the War Cross and the Medal of Honor. What a shame!

"A terrible shame, Colonel. My friend is a hero," Tsangarakis hesitantly ventured. But the colonel ignored him. He wanted to know in what battle zone the lieutenant had served. For how long? And under what circumstances was he decorated? Who was his commander? Who was his second-in-command? How was he wounded?

"He's a brave boy, Colonel. But modest you might say, a bit of a dumb John," Tsangarakis laughed protectively. But the colonel, not laughing, still wanted to know why after all Mr. Papaloukas hadn't entered the regular army? With his ability he could have a brilliant military career.

"A tremendous career, Colonel. Can you doubt it? But, with your permission, don't be discouraged. Even as a civilian he'll do well. Sound head, sound investment . . . we were childhood friends."

This time Tsangarakis was rewarded with a glance from the colonel, who also wanted to know how Mr. Papaloukas was a sound investment. The sharp and somewhat urgent correction by Mr. Papaloukas that he was just a student, in his last year at the Polytechnic School and not at all a sound investment, in absolutely no way a sound investment, made Tsangarakis laugh shamelessly. But the colonel's geniality unexpectedly increased.

"At the Polytechnic! Bravo, bravo! My boy, I wish you luck."

It was nevertheless obvious that he felt no professional or other interest. He was only a garrulous middle-aged traveler who didn't really want to know anything. He unbuttoned his shirt and loosened his belt. And the Governor of Preveza, Mr. Achilles Papaloukas, was he any relation? he asked out of boredom. But immediately a thunderous explosion:

"You don't say, my boy! Your father's brother! Old Achillakos your uncle!"

"Perfect!" Tsangarakis had barely time to exclaim. The colonel opened a bottomless bag of memories, marvelous memories, sentimental and voluptuous. Old Achillakos! What a great wonderful gentleman! Ah, ah, what wines, what parties they had, wild company, poker, hunting, fishing, once in Parga they had a feast, some patriotic holiday, eating and drinking three days. He then was director of ASVIP and Achillakos was Examiner of State Revenues for the Province of Thesproteia.

"Didn't I tell you, Colonel, it's a great family." Tsangarakis rubbed his hands, entranced.

"So, in Parga some chicks came over from the other side in men's trousers, some enchanting Corfiotes, and old Achillakos dived in head first. Ha! ha! ha! ho! ho!"

"He! he!" Tsangarakis echoed, stammering drunkenly, "Director! Inspector! Governor! I told you so, a great family."

Well then, many many kisses to his uncle from Colonel Karakitsos, his buddy Pamiko Karakitsos. They met ages ago before the civil war. Had old Achillakos aged any? The old lion didn't have a gray hair in his head! But me—just look! Mr. Karakitsos manfully stroked his thick white mane.

How could such a good-for-nothing grow old? Petros thought of the four hundred shares and the gold Napoleons in the jug, the common family inheritance from Grandmother which his uncle had embezzled . . . and the bad check he wrote a little later. Father generously made up the amount so that the thief, the embezzler, could stay out of jail. Certainly that thieving disgusting creature was involved in that mess. And just think, father was reduced to being a partner with the old fraud.

"I met your mother then too. Such a wonderful lady! So correct and highly educated." The colonel's enthusiasm spilled over.

Tsangarakis jumped up feverishly. "And his father, Colonel?"

"No, only the lady."

"He's a nobleman . . . a nobleman, Colonel, a five-star general!"

The colonel and the two lieutenants fixed their eyes on him, amazed.

"He won the war! Do you follow me, Colonel? What won the war is the roads, right? The roads were rebuilt according to a plan from headquarters, as you know. Well, and how many American dollars were laid out? They built thousands of miles of road so we could march anywhere. And then victory smiled on us. You as chief of staff can instruct us in depth in this matter."

"Yes, rebuilding the roads did play a certain role," the white head moved slowly, thoughtfully.

"The main role, Colonel! You as a military mind understand that. Well then, there you have Leonidas Papaloukas." He tapped Petros proudly on the knee. "My friend's father; we've been friends from childhood. In every road and bridge of this region, Leonidas Papaloukas as mastermind commanding general has the power to do what he likes."

Petros looked at him angrily and listened with care. That bum was well informed, he even knew Father's name, his position in the min-

istry . . . what more did he know? How he grinned shamelessly, like
a jackal. Big, yellow, predatory teeth with two gold ones in the middle.

In any case, the colonel was really sorry he never happened to
meet . . . he only met the lieutenant's mother, one summer years
ago when he was with ASVIP in Igoumenitsa. Old Achillakos was
looking after her then, and the poor man outdid himself. What an
aristocratic crowd they were in the evenings by the water! "I remember
that she had your little sister with her. A charming youngster, my
little daughter's age in fact."

At once the little daughter's photograph went around the compartment hierarchically from hand to hand. The colonel's grin reached
his ears. For his Amalitsa was, by the way, an A student. A few
days ago she graduated with straight A's from St. Joseph's School,
she knew beautiful French, and what an upbringing from her mama,
her watchful mama. The upbringing of a princess.

"With your permission, Colonel, she's truly a gazelle. But she's a
doll, a doll! You're a very lucky father." Tsangarakis' eyes bulged
the moment he grabbed the photo from the blond lieutenant.

Of course, he was a very lucky father . . . yes! yes! Suddenly the
colonel stumbled. Sure he was a lucky father. Just that the little bitch
insisted on going to the Polytechnic with those tall pimply-faced males.
The little bitch, her mama was going to murder her. But sweetheart
use your head, we're not rich, wrote the lucky father. What do you
want with that nonsense? Aren't there any good honest boys? In a
short time I'll be retiring.

Petros returned the photograph without a word. Outside the window
immense poplars were fleeing, then telephone poles again. The sun
had gone down, and on the low slopes the first shadows were gathering.
Mother had gone to Igoumenitsa right after the Occupation to sell
some lands she had inherited. The house was left bare during the
famine: furniture, rugs, books, and clothing turned into chickpeas,
gruel, olive oil. Petros was in his first year at the Polytechnic, and
mother wouldn't let him find a part-time job: a priest is a priest, and
a peasant a peasant. Father was still convalescing after surgery.
Thermopylitis is an incurable disease . . . poor Leonidas . . . the
worthless crook had ridiculed him behind their backs. Then he was

stealing government money, having made his loot during the Occupation selling boots to the Germans. During the Occupation he even proposed to Father a wild scheme involving all the small fortifications in Crete. Don't be poor and proud, he said, it's a fabulous windfall all neatly set up with General Hermann Kauber, a dirty job that would make the three of them filthy rich. Father, infuriated, threw him out of the house. That bloodsucker wouldn't stop even in his brother's hour of need, but connived with buyers and milked the profits from mother's properties in Igoumenitsa, as they were sold for what they could bring. Then Neneta was eleven, no twelve, beginning high school, now Father and that crook are partners with big plans, inseparable. Mother taking cardiograms and Neneta in despair . . . Here in his shirt pocket with the discharge papers is her last letter.

Alone at last.

Petros stopped at the window as they left the dining car. The lights had been on for a long time, dusk was deepening, and night was rushing down out of the wooded gorges of Olympos. But two steps ahead the colonel also stopped. He belched deeply with his hand on his stomach, his inflated cheeks like sacks of blood. He had emptied two bottles of wine, clinking glasses with Tsangarakis, who had also downed a liter, calling Petros a cheapskate because he wouldn't drink; he was swaying happily with the shaking of the train, a toothpick sticking out of his mouth.

"Hey, you disgusting gypsy." The colonel chewed his ass out, as if admiring him, and laughed. But as his great bulk bent over Petros a sudden shadow sobered him. "Let me ask you something, my boy. You have character, education." Suddenly he spun viciously around. "What are you up to, gypsy?"

Tsangarakis, frightened away, holed up in the compartment. The colonel's hand, hairy like a bear's paw, weighed despotically on Petros' shoulder. He waited indecisively for a conductor to pass by.

"You're from a fine family, Mr. Papaloukas. Tell me, damn it, what kind of school is this Polytechnic joint? They even teach drawing, who the hell heard of that? Imagine that little shit, rebelling against me!"

Petros barely restrained a smile. As a matter of fact they did teach art, he assured him, in the Polytechnic, in one of the schools of the Polytechnic. The colonel sighed and mopped his forehead; he couldn't believe it.

"A school, well, isn't that right? For them to teach you to paint. What will they tell me next! Ach, her mother will murder her." He belched hard and bent closer. "Forgive me, but as my best friend's little nephew I think of you as my son. Tell me, is that what they do in Paris? What should I do, eh?"

Petros had no time even to wonder.

"Lousy frogs! What do I care what they do or don't do in Paris?" grunted the colonel, who now had gotten his ideas mixed up, and again held up the huge checkered handkerchief and wheezed asthmatically. "Surprise . . . yes, my boy, I'll put my signature to that, surprise is not always the best tactic. What do you say?"

Petros said nothing, shrugged his shoulders. The sparks of the engine made sudden bright darts on the dark firmament and at once were gone. As they went over a small bridge an echo from the depths sounded for a moment. The lucky father was holding his head in his hands.

"The little bitch, ach! What can I do now? Her mother says she needs a whipping. Pamiko, wake up. Come out of your daze. You're right, you're perfectly right, I calm her down, just be patient and don't worry. I know what I'm going to do. 'Well, what will you do, stupid? Don't you understand? What can you do with that devil? Dear God, why did we have her? Come home quick!' her mother writes, 'quick or I'll cripple her.' That's why I'm going home now, to find out what's going on, and I'm in agony. I can't stand it. If I get home and she's not there . . .'"

There was no other way out for Petros. He locked himself in the toilet and smoked. Later, in the adjoining car, he lost himself at the open window. The train, all its lights ablaze, was fighting for its life in the night. Petros lit another cigarette. After all, by tomorrow he'd be home, this chaos would end, some common decision would be made. Still nine and a half hours. A village showed its few tiny lights from far away, flickering in the darkness, and vanished. And a third

cigarette. Petros' mouth tasted like poison, and the nightmarish heat
in the narrow aisle made him thirsty. Again his hand groped mechani-
cally for his breast pocket. Here were the discharge papers, and the
letter from Neneta, nearly in pieces from ten days' folding and unfold-
ing; Petros knew it almost by heart . . . The cup had run over and
what was the good of keeping it from Petros any longer, Neneta wrote
in despair. The poor girl had worked for so many months studying,
taking extra courses, and now she trembled with disappointment because today all of a sudden Father ripped up the books and notebooks
and wouldn't let her take entrance exams for the University. Medicine
is not for you, he said. What came over him so abruptly? And he'd
send her to Switzerland in the fall, he said, to some finishing school.
*But what good is Switzerland to me, Petros? And who'll take care
of Mother if I go? It's as if I were going crazy, our home is just
a monstrosity.* And Mother's mild sickness they had written him about
last winter, my God it was terrible. It wasn't dangerous, no, Mother
was in no danger, the cardiogram showed that her heart was physically
like iron, but sickness, horrible, one attack after another *and Father,
imagine, ridicules her and tells her to stop acting! As if we ever saw
Father. All his plans and schemes and the days he doesn't even come
home at night* . . . Tomorrow home, eight and a half more hours,
all this would have to be straightened out, no half-measures, no more
postponements. As long as you wore khaki you weren't responsible
somehow, Petros thought. But why didn't they write me this before?
Who would have imagined that everything would go to pieces so
quickly?

Tree shadows were black in the racing reflection of the train, and
night swallowed them up. The old pine tree rustled patiently in the
backyard on summer afternoons, always rustling outside the half-closed
shutter of his bedroom. Only eight hours still separated him from home,
from his bed, lying on his back in his undershirt in midsummer, that
friendly sound whispering to him as before . . . But now he was tired,
his legs worn out, and yet he couldn't stand to be cooped up in the
compartment again, wedged in between them. He paused at the doorway, indecisive, while the colonel laughed shatteringly, coughed, and
spat into his handkerchief.

"I don't believe you, you tramp! he roared, and stared fiercely at Tsangarakis.

"By the Holy Virgin, Colonel! The priest's wife gave me gonorrhea!"

"Not if you swear a thousand times . . ."

Tsangarakis, sweating all over as if infected, swore a thousand times, waved his arms, and talked, talked, talked, laughed, grimaced, poured ouzo out of a bottle into the colonel's cup, slapped the blond lieutenant on the back, poured him some ouzo too, drank some himself, *eviva!* and talked, talked, and everyone laughed aloud. No, Petros couldn't endure it, better on his feet in the corridor.

After an hour or so he came hesitantly back and looked in stealthily from the corridor. The noise had subsided but the light was still on. All the faces were stamped with deep melancholy as with a primeval seal: the bottle was empty. Tsangarakis was no longer talking, now only the colonel talked; he sighed heavily or grew angry and swore as he described to the mournful silent company what they do, what the hell they do in Paris. She says in Paris they barely poke their nose out of the egg, they're still hanging onto the tits, and bang! out the door. That's right, that's what they do, damn them in hell, decadent frogs! On the run to get jobs, you name it, secretaries, maids, factory girls, that is, whores. Don't you know all those filthy magazines where they photograph their naked asses? That's how they abandon the family, and abandon the principles of morality and religion, and get their own apartment, and live it up with five or six lovers and don't get married.

"Terrible," Tsangarakis remarked with the horror of a celibate priest.

"Myself I'd have all those unmarried women shot." The dark lieutenant pursed his lips malevolently. The blond one yawned.

Right! The colonel slammed his fist on his knee. They're the cause of worldwide corruption, let the world burn up! And then what does she say? "The women in Paris," she says, "are human beings and they don't treat them there like animals." Listen to me? I'm listening! Bah! he exclaimed, his voice cracking. That's what she tells you. "And in cultivated society the parties," she says, "go on all night, that's what they do." God damn what they do and don't do, it's almost six o'clock and where were you dragging your tail all night, you piece

of filth? "I'll do as I please," she says, "I'm a high-school graduate
now and I'm free." You're *what*, you say, free? So her mother grabs
her curls and slaps her down: tell me, or I'll kill you. And by God,
not a word, the slick hellion, not a tear, ack! And then she says with
such airs, "If you lift your hand against me again I'm leaving this
pigsty this very moment and reporting you to the District Attorney."
There you are, the immoral younger generation, rebellious vipers in
the bosom of the family. Hurry, she's sworn to dishonor you, the minx,
her mother writes frantically, come home quick, you're her father,
you take the responsibility. "Oh! Oh! What can I do now?" The colonel
hid his face in his hands and belched hopelessly.

"Be patient, Colonel," Tsangarakis resolved, after a moment's
thought. "She's a superb beauty, she'll be married soon and you'll
have some peace."

His idea provoked another unexpected explosion. The colonel showed
his fists again, trembling all over. For he'd just been thinking of the
matches she'd turned down, that godforsaken Albanian whore. Just
the other day, an obstetrician with a private practice in Koropi, and
a lieutenant, a boy with a heart of gold and what priority for promo-
tion, aide-de-camp to the division commander. It's driving him
crazy . . . fire, fire will burn the sinful world.

"You tell'em," Tsangarakis sighed.

"And now if I get home and she's not there. You know, there'll
be a Battle of Waterloo." He clenched his white head once more and
shut his eyes as if unable to gaze any longer at the chasm under
his feet. Utterly desolate, he whispered, "Well, so I . . . I agree; from
a tactical point of view surprise is nonsense. Why don't I call to say
I'm coming, ach!"

But now that he had dredged out everything inside him, his drinking
companions were tired of looking. They were bored, and anyway, it
was already eleven o'clock, and they were exhausted.

translated by Sarah Kafatou

Nights* TAKIS SINOPOULOS

I

An outing on Patission street, when there were thin pepper trees.

And steps heard beyond memory. Light from another century stays awake all night in the streetlamps.

When battalions of dreams, past and present, wall in a fragmentary life.

I won't stay here, I told you. An eye stares relentlessly behind the wall.

Attendant birds mark the night.

The small baby carriage.
The small girl they called Paula.
The small twig they called Ixel.
The small dental brace.

* from the poem "Chronicle"

And the broken hand.
And the black foot walking in an empty shoe.

Listen, said Konstantinos. There's the short guy we caught the other
day. I roped him to the bed. He was the masked informer in the
army camp. Put some water in the inkwell for him to drink and don't
hit him. We'll kill him later down in the weeds.

There were firing squads, fragments, in Parmenides, Empedokles, and
Heraklitos.

The people must fight.*

Guns, you told me, their shadow, the fear.

A mouth stitched into silence, not that hole that let in air when you
talked.

Plaster was chipping away inside his face. And chains of broken
images.

Thousands of packages, shitty truths in proper parcels, shapes, and
rhymed poems.

They arrested Peter.

They took Peter away in a white sheet down to his toenails.

And I told you about the blood.

And you spoke of power structures.

If you speak no one will hear.

* from Heraklitos, fragment 44.

Nights

II

Circular moonlight spirals around the earth.*

A light of stones, many pigeons on the windless roof.

Then Kroutagos ordered five hundred executed in the camp. At dawn they took them away. Only my dog escaped, you'll hear him howling in this maimed poem.

Workshops of silence, a gagged bell, when there is little in our land to mark days from nights.

That's why when you come from your house to the road, don't sing of having descended into Hell.

For the abyss goes on without you.

Later I told you, don't pull off the sheet. Under it, where his leg was, will be blackness.

Night with the hammering of night. Words dangling in air, a broken chain on the wall. From one room to the other.

Bilias, Polykarpos, and Katirtzoglou. And someone called Poretsanos. Like the road going down. A turn into the other world, Larisa in terrible half-light. On the left no cypresses in the ravine.

He had already been sanctioned. But what does sanctioned mean?

When from morning on, the wind keeps up.

They arrest you and drive a spike in your horizon.

The sun was on the balcony.

* from Empedokles, fragment 45.

55

Now things are still, frightening and still.

Thought is lighted through oblique cracks to forget the names.

And meetings, hushed voices, and that note you gave me, when
night was drunk with its own power.

When Bilias, Polykarpos, and that man Poretsanos. And the car at
the bottom of the hill where there was no trash. There they threw
the murdered corpses.

Below you could hear the waves, the sea.

A corner of light emerged from the sea. Or shall we say a holy offering
in the horrible story.

III

Wherever you look it's evil and only March. A chilling, poisoned light.

Wherever you look it's evil. And that other thing is constantly devised. So you can't breathe.

Only lies. And sandbags in mountainous piles. Freight cars bolted shut all night. And that other thing is constantly devised. So you can't breathe.

Rows of cells, and iron bars, barbed wire, and stakes. So you can't breathe.

One year, another year. Raw rotten times. How can you testify?

What answer can you get from that glaring plaster face? A frozen nightmare.

So talk and talk fast. Give us names and addresses. When did you meet by the well?

I know nothing. I am nothing, Nikitas said. I always slept in that hole you saw, filled with three hundred years of blood.

I'll give you what you want, Nikitas said. Except for the way downhill and the sandhills. It's my last image. Don't . . . don't.

We shall see.*

Be careful. Your children are wilting in this lousy climate, our father shouted.

Not a coin.

* from ancient Greek.

Of course, I said, it's madness to walk with your hands.

Also madness to kill with your hands.

Slowly the light slips away from the cypresses.

The knife darkens. The two-year-old bullet is sleeping on the shelf.

Tonight I stumbled again over Kimon's body.

Nights

IV

On the other side of the afternoon the sea is always sounding.

There is no afternoon, no sea.

Mrs. Iakovou. Sophia, I mean. Apartment four.

She appears at an upstairs window, closes something, draws the curtains. She has turned off the light. The window fades.

Those eyes were love, footpaths of lonely men.

Projections of darkness. The blind spot in a flashing movie sign.

More and more things for you to do,
more for yesterday,
remnants, leftovers,
more than ever before—absence. You go on lost.

Your life with your back against the wall and they frisk you.

Your life begins again in a new neighborhood and you were telling me:

Night agencies, you'll get away.

You'll come back naked, betrayed as before.

Tonight your teeth dig into the small piece of bitter bread where your freedom hides.

Tonight the stones open their windows.

A dark smile glides over what was once your mouth, your face.

Anonymous friend, you will sleep deep in an ancient bed.

59

If you only knew how all this started.

Old women walk about with dead children in their arms.

You stare at a nail on the wall, a jacket on it, shoes on the floor.

Moon on the balcony.

A house and endless houses.

And they tell you you'll get away, sign this.

Two men for a stretcher.

Two women for a kiss.

Four knives for the informer.

And for you the night.

And a dry tongue.

Someone with no name.

They pin you against the wall.

Then two men washing their hands

with water and soap.

V

Forty-four tractors.
Forty-five trucks.
Six rifles + eight.
Train at twelve we told them.
Train at two and seven-thirty.
Tuesday wednesday and wednesday afternoon.
Darkness.

And Sunday.
More darkness.

Hello, Mr. Iakove, hello.

The man shuffling cards at the next table, mask on, his glittering
hands, teeth, smile, smile, a friend.

You know who is talking, you don't know who he is.

The black footpath is a pier to memory. The shattered streetlamp with
the bulb knocked out. This stone wall is a shantytown for the new
corpses.

Dry reports, dry postscripts.

Traps, snares, and trap doors which you didn't know, trees and half-
dark firing squads, the last defiant cry.

As we talked, Nikitas suddenly got up in the middle of the room,
grabbing his head like a madman, his head caught fire, spitting out
stones and iron. Then ashes. He cools off, and sits down again,
speechless.

Later the new bosses, the swastika torturers, safety on its knees,
mutilated, not only in appearance.*

* *not only in appearance*, from ancient Greek.

Takis Sinopoulos

Then that quick laughter like a splintering glass.

Then a battered wall, iron rings on the wall, the brain a soft, soaked bloody sponge.

Guilt of the guilty, guilt of the innocent.

Slaughter of the innocent, the lie and again the lie, truth, lie, then night, sleep, sleep.

You'll forget them, you'll forget everything.

Years will sweep you away too, trash.

As always in history a fiendish wind blows.

Monuments of silence where people have no water.

The great visions of man.

Roads and dirt roads, rickety hovels, and beyond, the dark, immobile banks.

Further back a very sharp knife. Stab your friend on the secret footpath,

Get your friend in the back. He gapes wildly as he caves to the floor.

Horrifying reports, horrifying meanings.

Iron slogans, dregs of darkness in your doglike head.

Dregs of love, just words,

like words,

In this acid poem that suddenly turns and bites its tail.

translated by Willis Barnstone

A Testimony   NORA ANAGNOSTAKIS

What do you think? how long will this business go on? on the one hand,
a whole people speaking in a certain manner, and on the other, a handful
of people hoping to make the people speak *their* language!—
Dionysios Solomos

In the spring of 1967 I was about to have a book published, contain-
ing essays on poetry, fiction, contemporary trends, and so on.

The book was not published; but the manuscript and notes remained.
I was glancing through them the other day, with a certain amount
of curiosity, trying to see what could be salvaged for the reader of
today, and for myself.

A few crumbs remain.

Amid the scholarly, high-sounding stuff, I found this strange note:
"In the kingdom of the mute, only a poetry of gestures will flower;
the criticism of that poetry will be a criticism of pantomime." I was
struck by the relevance of this observation, and decided to use it.

I hadn't written a line in three years, so I thought I would try
now. I had grown completely estranged from such things as writing
paper and pencils, from the tyrannies and delights of self-expression.
I had come to feel, perhaps naively, that these things were useless,
irreverent, and inaccessible, since we did not even have the right to
speak as we wished. I still believe that a restrictive use of language

cannot possibly give birth to living literature. Whether or not it is necessary and useful to keep language alive simply for the elementary requirements of survival is another matter. Only great craftsmen can do something about it, but again, how often, and for how long?

However, since I was given even this limited opportunity, I felt duty-bound to test the capacities and courage of my tongue. One uses what one has. Within the stifling framework of moderation (which does not mean wisdom), I found I had to push across the page words that were absolutely concrete, stripped of allegory, symbol, satire, myth—all those devices which literature, even in better days, uses freely to enrich—but not smother—expression.

No works of literature worthy of the name had appeared recently to write about. It was indeed true that the only poetry that "flowered" during these three years was the gestures of certain persons. These gestures kept alive the morale, the virtue, the faith, the entire, living, spiritual tradition of the country. There was nothing beyond that I really wanted to say; and aesthetic problems had ceased to interest me.

What could I write about then?

Without quite knowing what lay ahead, I thought I would just try.

I had to begin somewhere. So on a clean page I wrote down the brief passage I mentioned before; I needed something to lean on, and then, I would wait and see. Empirical procedures. My first mistake, I soon found out, was trying to talk about the present with words from another era. I paid dearly for this false loan. But come to think of it, I drew some benefit from it after all. I don't remember how that brief passage happened to be written, but I remember *when* it was written. In those days our blissful state of expressive freedom gave me the intoxicating ability to see the course of poetry unhindered even by the most unfavorable circumstances. A vestige of memory, it seems, warned my mind, while refusing to assume the form of an actual menace and disrupt my beatific mood. The rather elegant and lighthearted style, the slightly raised tone of voice in that short passage not only did not denote any real anxiety, but betrayed a certain complacence. The verb "flower," in particular, seemed to emphasize the superior standing of poetry even under such circumstances, as compared to simply shutting up, and the importance of even such a reduced function as the criticism of pantomime as compared to the everyday motions of the mute in his miserable efforts at elementary communication; in short, as compared to his vegetable life.

Today, I would be ashamed to use the word "flower." The only verb that comes to my mind is "maintain," or "keep alive" (glancing back at what I have written, I can confirm this). Other words I have just used are: "shutting up" and "vegetable life," so anyone idle and interested enough to delve into the criticism of pantomime may draw his own conclusions. Words carry a ponderous weight, and if we are not careful how we handle them, they may fall over and crush us. In the old days, the observation about the kingdom of the mute was true, because it was supported by facts and conditions, and by my own carefree frame of mind. But now that this ghost of an observation has taken on the flesh and bones of actuality, its words ring in my ear with a false and hollow sound.

I refused to listen to this sound, and here is how other words—springing from the heart of reality—answered it. My second observation—in reality my first—was: "For those whose gestures are too 'poetic,' there are always laws and authorities to bind or cut off their hands."

So academicism is answered with sarcasm. The style has become brusque and harsh, the tone of voice realistic and caustic, the words speak of present concrete things. And, most characteristic, the tense of the verbs automatically changes. We suddenly switch to the present.

Between those two observations lies the same gap that separates words describing a precipice from the precipice itself.

After this, a moment of utter helplessness. How am I to get out of this mess? Petrified, I stare at the two passages; they hypnotize me. I was not fully aware of the trap I let myself into. So I got caught, clever bird that I was.

Then along came a third note: "Why so much confusion? What has poetry to do with authority? How did this initial observation, concerning the 'flowering' of poetry, come to founder so soon in condemnations and punishments? Are things not working properly, or is thought not working properly? Or do they proceed hand in hand and therefore work beautifully?"

Things were functioning beautifully. Only my mind was confused. What was I trying to do? Was I attempting to reveal, to highlight the dramatic reality of our true condition by this device of hypocritical ignorance and query, by cheap conjuring tricks with words? ("We can no longer earn our living with our work, but only through cunning," I immediately wrote in the margin.) Presenting this case, the most important I ever had had to defend, I found I had already made a compromise, like the clumsiest, most amateurish of lawyers. How could I say these things? Whom was I talking to? Was I indulging in cheap journalism? Suddenly I was seized by a kind of arrogance. My means, my responsibilities, my targets should be quite different. Then why had I allowed myself to speak like a third-rate columnist? Was it accidental? Not at all. I had merely been imitating the only style of writing in existence at present, the style we encounter every day in the newspapers—nowhere else. Such mishaps are necessary "to teach us humility," as the wise teacher said, and to check our conceit and pitiful self-importance in the midst of our inaction, as we rely on pompous words like "mission" and "responsibility," while others carry on with their job, whatever it might be, the best they can. (I notice I have been using the first-person plural.)

I felt the need to justify myself. And so the fourth note: "In the turmoil of the times, with this aching inside me, with so much to say that I cannot possibly say, with my tongue so numb under constant pressure to weigh each single word and its consequences in the balance, I have finally lost the conscientiousness, the humanity of my language. From the very beginning, I have been obsessed by the thought of how best to disguise my language, what form to choose to say what I have to say. For I have something to say; but I cannot say it without cheating, without tricks. I am filled with fear and passion. What kind of truth can I articulate in this condition? I am, literally, speechless."

Now, for the first time, I discern a breath of life in the pitiful sincerity of my words. I notice that I have used words I respect, words I fear, words I do not handle easily, even in everyday speech: humanity, conscientiousness, sincerity. Qualities I would like to possess, though I don't know whether I have any claim to them. From this attempt at justification, it seems that the scales I held had passion and fear on one side and a desperate will to do my duty on the other. Probably the effort to balance the scales has failed purely as a result of personal inadequacy. I have had to go through great upheavals to arrive at this flattened tone of voice, this poor mutilated text, a thousand times scissored, full of holes—the most difficult I have ever written.

It occurs to me that the labors of duty, like those of decay, reach fruition slowly and are the work of a lifetime.

I wanted to show that I have tried. I wrote what I wrote as a simple testimony of self-criticism.

For today, then, I submit this broken gesture, these defeated words. For tomorrow, we'll see.

translated by Kay Cicellis

The Candidate RODIS ROUFOS

to Gustavo Durán *in memoriam*

The summons with the letterhead "Policía, Dirección de Seguridad," ordered him to report at 10:30 A.M. to Lieutenant Ramón Morales, room 35, for a loyalty check. There was no address, but none was needed. Everyone in Anunciación, in all Boliguay for that matter, knows the secret police headquarters is located (symbolically, according to some venomous tongues) at the corner of the Plaza de la Revolución—formerly Plaza de la Libertad—and the Avenida de los Estados Unidos.

Room 35 was just a dark anteroom. "Wait here," a clerk told him after a perfunctory glance at the summons. "Señor Morales is busy."

The officer's name sounded familiar, but Juan couldn't place it. He tried to relax on the hard seat and again confront the traditional slow ways of bureaucracy, which no threatening directive from the Junta had managed to change. Thank God, he thought, this was the last formality between him and the chair in organic chemistry. Once the secret police issued him a loyalty certificate, giving him clearance as a candidate, the faculty was practically bound to elect him. No other lecturer (since Alejo was out of it) had the qualifications to succeed the distinguished old professor who was fired in the purge at the University soon after the *pronunciamento* and the establishment of the dictatorship.

At 11:15 Juan began to feel that the officer was overdoing it. It was not in his character to complain, however. Alejo had often attacked him good-naturedly about his timidity, probably inherited from long generations of poor villagers who trembled before any authority. "Why let them step on you," he would say. "Tell them to go to hell!" Alejo would long since have stalked out of the office, slamming the door. Juan compromised, promising himself he would wait till 11:30, not a second longer.

He couldn't help thinking about Alejo Prieto, his closest friend; they had grown up together, studied together, and both joined the faculty. Though a superb researcher and teacher, Alejo had refused two months earlier to submit his candidacy for the chair and tried hard to persuade Juan to do likewise. He made passionate speeches against the regime— without even bothering to lower his voice, the madman—and used melodramatic exaggerations like "to get a position today you have to sell your soul." Finally they parted very upset with each other, even more so than when Alejo had spoken of his involvement in an illegal student network and Juan upbraided him sharply over it. That was their last conversation. A few days later Alejo was deported to a remote village in the Cordillera and deprived of his faculty post. They claimed he had tried to conceal students wanted by the secret police in connection with that huge *Viva la Democracia* chalked on the University wall.

His friend's misfortune saddened Juan but did not change his mind. He simply was not interested in politics. Whatever the regime, someone had to teach organic chemistry to the students. True, they didn't seem to share his view. As soon as his candidacy for the chair became known, students who till then had smiled warmly at him—how shallow and unstable young people were!—began to treat him with icy formality. It was good that Alejo, stubborn as he was, didn't hold a grudge. That very morning a letter from him had come, from Pueblo Viejo, hand-carried, and a quick glance told Juan that there was no mention of the University or their quarrels. He had put it in his pocket to read later, carefully. Not now of course at Security headquarters. It would be foolish, even dangerous, to be found reading a message from an enemy of the regime, especially uncensored. For similar reasons he had not yet gone to see Alejo in his village.

It was 11:28 when they led him into a large, sunny room, cheerfully decorated with colored pictures of national monuments and the Leader's slogans inscribed on yellow-green Boliguayan flags. An entire wall was occupied by the familiar enormous poster depicting the Revolution (a fierce young virgin holding a sword and Bible), surrounded by the Armed Forces (a tank, warship, and airplane) and the People (peasants in traditional poncho and sombrero, smiling beatifically), in the act of slaying a red many-headed dragon labeled "Castrismo, Anarquía, Corrupción" and rescuing from its talons a middle-aged lady, "Boliguay Católico." Behind the officer's desk hung the portrait of President Alvarez in full dress, with three rows of metals and a cheerful smile which indicated that the picture had been taken before the titular Head of State went, disappointed, into voluntary exile in Montevideo.

Ramón Morales was a tall, athletic man of about thirty-five who wore civilian clothes like a tailor's mannequin. A lavish application of scented brilliantine made his black hair glisten almost as brightly as his numerous gold teeth. He received Juan with great courtesy, apologizing for the delay, directed him to a comfortable chair, offered him a cigarette, and asked what he would like to drink. Then he sat down at his desk and said he was sorry he had to submit the Señor Lecturer to this inconvenience, but it was unfortunately required for the issuance of a loyalty certificate.

"Just a formality, you understand," he explained with a polite smile. "At the same time, I'm delighted to have the opportunity and the honor of making the acquaintance of a scientist of your distinction."

Charmed by the officer's manners (how unfair the fanatic opponents of the regime were to these people), Juan replied that the pleasure was his, and that he was eager to provide whatever information the police judged useful!

In the beginning the questions dealt with family background, career, and trips abroad. Every now and then Morales consulted a thick file. Juan regretted, a bit sleepily, that he had ordered coke, not coffee.

"So you did postdoctoral work at Princeton University from 1958 to 1961. Did you travel anywhere else during that time?"

"No."

"Curious. According to our data, you visited Havana in 1960, from the 7th to the 11th of October."

A change in the tone of the officer's voice jerked Juan out of his drowsiness and made him sit up.

"Ah, of course. The Panamerican Biochemical Conference. I beg your pardon, it slipped my mind."

"Naturally, naturally. And what were your impressions of Cuba?"

Juan shrugged his shoulders. "I stayed a very short time, you know, and I was very busy. There were official receptions, an evening of folk dances. I had no time to study local conditions, and frankly I wasn't interested in them."

The officer patted his hair, releasing a wave of scent. He said pensively as though with regret:

"Then your impressions were not unfavorable?"

A bit ruffled, Juan nonetheless thought it wise to humor his examiner's mood.

"I can't say that," he offered cautiously. "Some consumer goods were unobtainable, and the service at the hotel was mediocre."

"Ah!" murmured Morales approvingly, as if giving Juan a good grade. "Lack of consumer goods and services—yes, those are classical signs of a Communist regime. But what about the crucial ones, the lack of freedom, and atheism?"

"Perhaps I would have observed these too if I had remained longer," Juan answered a little drily. "But why do you dwell on that short trip? Surely it doesn't make me suspect, does it?"

He laughed at his own suggestion, to show how preposterous it was. But his laughter did not have the hearty ring he intended, and the policeman didn't join in. At that moment they brought Juan his coke, and he was relieved at the interruption. A few seconds later the officer passed his hand again over his immaculate coiffure, sighed audibly, and went on.

"You are a close friend of Alejo Prieto, aren't you?"

Juan felt himself reddening and resented it. He slowly lit a cigarette and forced himself to look the officer in the eye.

"We've known each other for many years," he answered, "and we have always been on good terms." He stopped short and then, feeling inexplicably guilty, added, "we didn't agree about everything, of course."

His hope that this would be enough was wrong. The officer pounced on the last words.

"Ah! Did you, for instance, disagree on politics?"

"Yes," Juan replied with some hesitation.

"Meaning?"

"Well, I voted Conservative and he voted Liberal."

The officer beamed at him. "I'm happy to hear it. Conservatives are the natural supporters of the Revolution. You are aware, of course, that Señor Prieto is a dangerous character?"

"I know that he was deported on that charge."

The officer cast him a penetrating glance.

"What difference is there? Do you think we make mistakes in such matters?"

Juan groped uneasily for the correct answer.

"I am certain," he said slowly, "that you do your best to avoid mistakes."

"Kindly stop hedging!" the officer snapped unexpectedly. "Are you or are you not convinced that your friend is a danger to public security?"

Juan made a weary gesture, as if hoisting a white flag. "All right," he said sadly. "Let's say he is. What does that have to do with me?"

The officer again assumed his ingratiating tone.

"We'll see about that," he said smiling. "Now tell me your opinion of our Catholic government."

Juan had expected this question. Knowing it would be an error to show hesitation, he had prepared an answer which would be neither compromising nor untrue.

"As I understand it, its purpose is to return the country to true democracy. I am wholly in accord with that program."

The officer grimaced.

"Come now, Señor, that is unworthy of a man like yourself."

"I beg your pardon!" Juan exclaimed, astonished.

"You know very well what I mean. Forget what you read in the newspapers, and let's speak frankly. I want a straight answer—are you with us or not?"

Juan began to panic. The conversation was not going at all as he had expected.

"I don't understand," he complained. "I thought you were making a routine loyalty check. You told me so yourself."

"So what?" The officer, no longer smiling.

"I have always been a law-abiding citizen. I don't meddle in politics, but I've been consistently opposed to Communism. What more do you want?"

Morales assumed the expression of a long-suffering father about to admonish a much loved but naughty child. He pulled a sheet out of the file, saying,

"Here is a report on you."

He began to read in a loud voice. After two or three sentences Juan stared at him with amazement that gradually turned to indignation and then despair. The text characterized him as a "leftist," "a person with anarchistic tendencies," who praised Cuba, insulted the regime, and slandered the Army. Some of the accusations were based somewhat on actual events, but exaggerated and misinterpreted in a completely irrational way—it was as though he were peering at himself in a trick mirror at an amusement park and being told that the grotesque image was his real self. It was true, for example, that on learning of the expulsion of his predecessor he had expressed regret and asked his colleagues, mostly for appearances' sake, whether they could do anything for him. This was interpreted as "an attempt to incite University personnel to an illegal strike or mutiny." In a scientific article he had referred with praise to the views of a Polish biophysicist. This was described as "propaganda for the alleged achievements of Communist scientists." And so forth.

As he finished, the officer gave his visitor a funereal glance.

"Well?" he said.

Juan weighed him, and decided he was trustworthy and capable of recognizing the truth if it were presented to him rationally and clearly. So he drew together all his courage and threw himself into refuting the accusations point by point. He spoke calmly, controlling his nervousness, and, as he watched the officer nod every now and then as if in assent, his hopes flew up again. Without realizing it, Juan at that time was drawing a portrait of himself. From his words emerged the image of a self-made, hard-working man devoted exclusively to his discipline, but also of an upright citizen, keen on law and order, distrustful of all social change, who voted the right way, eager to accept whatever officialdom told him, if it were not too fantastic. Gradually Morales' gold teeth were bared again in friendship.

"All right," the officer said unexpectedly, as Juan paused to catch his breath. "All right. I know those accusations are ridiculous."

Juan was struck dumb, his mouth gaped. Drops of sweat ran down his forehead. "But then why—why?" he whispered after a minute. As he received no immediate reply, his bewilderment turned to anger. "Why did you read those things to me if you knew they were lies?" he demanded. "And who said all that about me? I want his name, I'll sue him!"

The officer looked amused.

"Come now, Señor," he said soothingly. "We can't disclose our sources. You will find out why I read it to you in a little while. And now tell me, you consider yourself a loyal citizen, don't you?"

"Certainly," Juan said with self-assurance. His anger had already evaporated. It was a psychological test, he thought, and I passed it successfully.

"Ah!" said Morales, doodling with a pencil without looking at him. "But loyal to whom?"

"Why, to—to the State—the Constitution . . ."

The officer shook his head disapprovingly, like an examiner who is dissatisfied with the examinee's answers. "Caballero, the meaning of loyalty has changed since the Revolution." He stopped doodling, came forward, and sat on the edge of the desk nearest Juan.

"Yes," he continued, "it has changed. In the past, anyone who was not a Communist was considered a good citizen, eligible for the University. The result is that the University is full of people calling them-

selves Conservatives or Liberals or politically neutral, and who have
one thing in common: they don't give a damn about the Revolution.
Isn't that so?"

"But the purge . . ."

"The purge hit only a few of our most outspoken opponents. Even
now the majority of the professors are indifferent, not to mention the
lecturers and assistants." His voice grew harsh, the words whistled
like bullwhips. "Your colleagues are like all intellectuals. They resent
censorship, and because they don't understand the danger of Castroism
they are secretly yearning for the old system. But that"—every syllable
was a hammer-stroke—"we will no longer tolerate. Indifference and
neutrality are not good enough for us, do you understand? Not good
enough in the University or anywhere else." He leaned toward Juan,
his face crimson. "From now on, whoever is not with us is against
us. Today I wouldn't give a loyalty certificate even to him!"

With a dramatic gesture he pointed his pencil at the portrait of
Alvarez. Juan was shocked into silence. Reverence for the lawful Head
of State was an integral part of his conservative faith. As though
soothed by his own outburst, the officer proceeded more calmly:

"By insisting on unconditional loyalty to our Catholic government,
we may deprive the University of some top men. It doesn't matter.
If first-rate men are not politically reliable, we'll get second- and third-
rate men. Faith in the Revolution is more important than any theoretical training for those who are to educate the youth. As a candidate
for a chair, you will have to accept that and take the consequences."

Juan's mouth was dry. Some of Alejo's remarks in their last conversation flitted through his consciousness like mocking insects: "An insult
to human dignity," "To sell your very soul . . ." He swallowed twice.

"What consequences?" he managed at last to ask in a casual voice.

"I'll tell you, because I like to be honest. If you are to be a professor
you must first of all agree that your teaching will always be in accordance with healthy Boliguayan Catholic principles and the ideals
of the Revolution."

A few years before, Juan had reluctantly allowed Alejo to drag
him to an avant-garde French play. The spectacle had justified his

worst apprehensions. The plot was illogical and the characters talked
at cross-purposes. He now felt just like one of them.

"But I teach organic chemistry!" he almost shouted. "Don't you
see that it's a discipline with no place for ideology?"

"Never mind that," the officer assured him. "There will be plenty
of other opportunities. Your duties will not be confined to teaching
your subject. You will help, for example, with the enlightenment of
the rural population. You will go to the villages and explain to the
inhabitants the meaning of the Revolution. You will also speak on
the subject to your students, on appropriate occasions."

"But I don't know how to make political speeches!"

"They won't be political, they'll be patriotic. However, don't worry,
we'll give them to you written out, you won't have to do anything
but read them. Apart from that, of course, you will follow any instructions you receive. For example, you will vote to expel any student
who is considered undesirable."

"Undesirable for what reason?"

Juan knew the question was naive, but he was desperately playing
for time. The officer looked at him coldly.

"For whatever reason we consider sufficient," he answered sharply.
"There will be no discussion, do you understand?"

Juan nodded his head affirmatively. Yes, now he understood a great
deal—as if a dazzling light suddenly illuminated a misty realm he
had never before dared to look at. Now there was no further need
to play for time; he could relax.

"It goes without saying," continued the officer, "that you will report
any unlawful action that comes to your attention."

"Such as arson, theft, murder?"

So rarely did Juan use sarcasm, so unaccustomed were the muscles
of his face to expressing it, that it took no effort for him to keep
a perfectly straight face. Usually people were fooled by it, and
imagined some misunderstanding; but Morales understood and flushed
red.

"You know very well what I mean!" he roared angrily.

He regained his self-control at once, however, and even managed

a smile as he added, "Subversive activities are as unlawful as murder
and arson, and more likely to occur in the University. It will be your
duty to report them. Otherwise you will become their accomplice—like
your friend Señor Prieto. By the way, I'm told that many students
are complaining about his dismissal. You will have to talk to them,
to explain how antinational his behavior was."

He uttered the last words in a careless tone, but his glance was
fixed searchingly on his visitor as he paused to let them sink in. Then
he said quietly.

"That is what we mean, today, by loyalty. Are you prepared to
accept the terms?"

Juan did not look àt him for a while. He was reflecting silently
on the dream which had accompanied him through the first difficult
student years—the ambition to become some day a professor at the
University of Anunciación. In theory, he was still free to choose; in
reality, the decision had already been taken by some other self awakened by that dazzling light: a new, hitherto unknown Juan breathing
freedom and anger. "Tell him to go to hell," this new being seemed
to whisper in his ear. "It's now or never."

He stood up and turned determinedly toward the officer. Morales
stood up as well, more casually; there was cool, speculative amusement
in his eyes as he awaited the other's reaction. At this critical moment,
though, Juan suddenly felt he was losing his nerve—as had happened
once before, in his youth, in front of an overseer of the United Tomato
Company, who had insulted him before the entire village. That man
was just like Morales: well-groomed, insolent, sure of his power. Juan
was not cut out for imposing stances and gestures; he would have
made himself completely ridiculous by starting a quarrel with a man
a head taller than himself. Beneath the policeman's oily hair and
affected manners lurked—how had he failed to spot it from the beginning?—an old back-street bully who now had found a legal outlet
for his instincts. He remembered suddenly why the name Ramón
Morales seemed familiar: he had heard it often whispered with terror
at the University in connection with arrests, with persecutions of every
kind, with beatings of students, and with other, much worse things

The Candidate

which people hardly dared allude to—like that suicide of a professor
of plant pathology, the year before . . .

Almost sick with fear and nausea, cursing his cowardice, Juan was
unable to utter a word. The other man helped him.

"So the answer is no, then? I thought so." He nodded his head
knowingly. "I knew it even before meeting you. But to be correct
I had to give you the opportunity to choose."

For a moment Juan forgot both his irritation and the unpleasant
thought which had just occurred to him—that now even his position
as Lecturer was in jeopardy.

"How did you know?" he asked in naive wonder.

"The officer smiled condescendingly, obviously pleased, and tapped
him familiarly on the arm.

"Experience," he said, "has taught us that reports like the one I
read to you, even when mistaken in some details, are seldom wrong
in their general findings. You may not have done a thing you are
accused of, but all the same you are not a man we can use. That's
why I made the conditions sound stricter than they would actually
be: so that you would refuse now. It saves trouble for both of us later
on. It would not have been necessary, for example, for you to report
subversive activities of students. We know about them and follow them
closely enough. But what does count is that you did not like the idea
of reporting them to us—that alone shows you are not on our side.
It's a shame," he added politely, "the students will have a less distinguished professor. Good day."

Juan did not even realize how he happened to be, a while later,
in a bar on the Paseo Bolívar drinking strong pisco—something he
had never done at that time of day. Later, walking in the Public Gar-
den, he felt a mixture of irrational perplexity and bitter loneliness
seeing that nothing had changed: carefree people were strolling about,
pensioners sat in the cool shade, mothers yelled after their children,
couples whispered into each other's ears. No one, not one of all these
people appeared to guess what was happening in Boliguay, or to care—
not even a gang of young men and girls who went by with laughter
and a soft song. Juan suddenly realized he was dragging his feet in

79

exhaustion. He sat on a bench and felt in his pocket for cigarettes, but instead found a paper, Alejo's letter. With a thrill of expectation, like a thirsty animal that smells water, he began to read it again:

". . . The local peasants fear the policeman, and don't speak to me in his presence. He himself is a kind man, but is afraid to show me sympathy for fear some informer might report him to his superiors. Now I understand the working of that chain of terror which allows a small gang of conspirators to keep an entire people enslaved against its will . . .

"And yet life in Pueblo Viejo has taught me the other, the lovable aspect of this people. These same terrorized peasants do everything they can, in secret, to stand by me—with a smile, a few words quickly muttered as they walk by, a basket of food left at night outside my door . . . and the wretches are so poor! The fruit, the wild game they bring are princely gifts both for them and for me.

"One of the poorest is Pedro, the village simpleton, who supports himself by odd jobs and errands. Yesterday he brought me from the Post Office a card from Chiquita, with nothing on it but the lines of Luis Cernuda: "The revolution is reborn perpetually, a fiery phoenix, in the hearts of the disinherited . . ." and underneath the word "Courage!" I must have shown my feelings, because Pedro said to me, "Caballero, I want you to do me a favor." I supposed he wanted money, and it was hard because I didn't even have ten pesos with me, but he went on, "do me a favor, Don Alejo, and stop worrying. All this will pass!" And with a sweeping gesture he made me understand that "all this" included my exile, the dictatorship, and the whole black fortune of our country.

"I spoke to you once of Chiquita (that evening in January, when we disagreed). If you meet her—I know you'll like her, even if you were reluctant then—kiss her for me and tell her to be careful. As for me, I won't lose my courage. Pedro is right. Our people have seen so very much in their history! This too will pass."

Juan wiped his clouded glasses carefully and smiled. Of course he remembered who Chiquita was, and now was impatient to meet and to help her. But only Alejo could tell him how to find her. He had to go and see him at once in Pueblo Viejo.

All his initial exhaustion and bitterness disappeared as he set out,
walking quickly to the nearest travel agency. In the street he met
the same group of young people, and this time an unknown love, a
warm hope was in his blood. Maybe these laughing youths also be-
longed to "Chiquita"—as they affectionately called the illegal network
of democratic students . . .

translated by Rodis Roufos and Sarah Kafatou

Dr. Ineotis GEORGE HIMONAS

1

Suddenly the new species of man a distinct species is about to come.
A new and absolute race unimaginably perfect. The frightened people
of the past must vanish. Arrangements have been made for them to
die on a certain day. But each must return to his native village and
die there. Dr. Ineotis goes out and joins in with the people. His companion is a gypsy knife grinder. When the time came for them to
die they learned they were not to die a natural and painless death
as they had been told. But like a punishment a calculated death by
torture.

2

In the morning the people went off to die as they were told. They
had been ordered to return to die in the towns and rainy villages
where they were registered. As in a public census all were to die
on a specific date and in their legal residence. Greece was in turmoil.
But with no crying or anger. Rather with fear and miserable silence.
Families came out into the streets and were on their way. Just then
Dr. Ineotis saw the blond excrement of small children at the edge

* These first three episodes are excerpts from a book published in 1971.

83

of the road and began to sob. He imagined their glittering intestines
and organs turned into dried skin under the motionless sun and said
*I am too sentimental and anyway I couldn't live any longer I had
to die* and then he cried out to the mob like a maniacal prophet shouting
that it was not an injustice and that our death was necessary because
of the new species. He walks and dances and walks with the people
and next to the knife grinder. Ineotis' companion was a neighborhood
gypsy, carrying his grindstone on his back they are always together.
The trip took a day and a night. On the appointed day at dawn the
people reached the place of death. They pitched tents and lit small
white fires and the sky was white like a throat and the people waited.
Then came the news and they realized they had been tricked were
trapped. They learned that they were not to die in a natural way
as in sleep as promised but in a horrifying manner. Raging madmen
would tear them to pieces and burn them alive and rip out their bowels
with rusty crowbars with those savage iron rods left about abandoned
railroad stations. A cruel but just punishment. They all turned their
heads and stared at him frightened plaintively they turned and stared
plaintively at Dr. Ineotis.

3

For five hours Dr. Ineotis bowed his head and stared at his hands.
Suddenly he raised his head. The angels gathered at the open door
looking at him. Angels are all those things he won't say and won't
find and won't know they don't fit into his whole troubled life and
won't disappear. They might never have been—yet were incubating
long ago and now were crowding the corridors filling the stairway
the empty hospital and reached the ledge of the seven towers. Their
wings shivering but unflapping dirty with dust and lime. Angels are
not

yet angels are

dark but youthful fathers

white over white and burnt over burnt over the white pits with burnt

eyes he watches the men despairingly yet defiantly watches the men.
No man is worthy of me. Men are human fragments. Hanging rotating
very slowly with a layer of thick fat from an unknown fish to shield
them from the unbearable cold and multicolored from a light. At night
he was cold and dreamt of a fire he seized the fire puts it on his
head and on his belly with frozen ashes on his face he wanders about
at night when glands rupture from an old disease one or two hours
after midnight when swollen boils and great blisters burst and drain
he stretches and leans on the low surrounding mountains he runs into
the bushes and their avenging branches tufts of hair from the dread
laughing head of the racing god that's the direction of his whole life
and Dr. Ineotis always wears black and a silver chain and the dark
gypsy knife grinder is cheerful but mute. He saw the people who
were about to die but how could he speak to them and inform them
since great truths are like alien souls. But cheerful and somewhat sly
he joined the departing crowd. The knife grinder at his side. They
were walking in the sun and he remembered an old incident that
took place in a huge deserted airport. At that time it impressed him
deeply and he felt sick and remembered it now because of the sun.
He was with six men but they left him on the asphalt road and went
inside the deserted airport. They climbed up on a tractor and started
it. He stayed on the road and they drove the tractor onto the runway.
They shouted and the sun was hot and blinding. One of the girls
was lame and small as if stunted and wore big dangling blue earrings
that glowed in the sun. They drove to the center of the runway and
were engulfed by the heavy sun and disappeared a hundred meters
away from him and he stayed at the edge of the airport shuddering
and felt deep inside him their disappearance into the sun as they too
must have felt it on the tractor as they roared away and he even
thought he heard them being sucked away. A story of a tremendous
love, a sun-woman who fell in love with someone. The irises of her
eyes were reddish she came from Beirut. They had thrown her out
because of some story connected with the evil eye. She loved him
and swallowed him up like that sun and no matter how he struggled
and no matter what he did he could not escape and she swallowed
him like a bright hole and not passionately but frozen and speechless

and maybe sorrowfully her red eyes burnt him from afar like the
sun. Along the road a young man was dying from an unknown cause
and Dr. Ineotis leaned over him a woman was crying and saying
no no my boy tomorrow no not till tomorrow and suddenly a man
lunged forward and seized the young man dragging him brutally by
the feet dragging him along the road and shouted furiously and with
tears and impassioned hatred for certain people he cried *it's for tomorrow not today get up*. Then he left him right there and ran off the
road till he fell on his face. Dr. Ineotis leaned over the young man
who was dying and with peculiar malice but also fanatic enthusiasm
he told him *they will not be like us a terrible change has taken place
called cosmo-Iberian and they may even have different bodies* Dr.
Ineotis thought and a deep melancholy oppressed his heart as if he
were fainting and a piercing terror seized him because he sensed how
definitive and final his end would be. Toward evening they reached
a river and spent the night there. All at once a multitude of people
began to emerge from the still waters and they flooded up along the
shore. The man was a mournful soldier but the woman was very gay.
Her gaiety shone through her silence. In everyday life she must have
been one of those young women who are always lively and cheerful
and laugh at anything and tease everybody. They go into fits of laughter and have to hang onto a door not to fall over from laughing and
step back from the window hiding their bright faces in their hands.
Dr. Ineotis shuddered. Somewhere in the night Tenagne blazed and
went out. Tenagne is a naked snow-white woman with long black
hair. She is very beautiful and always crouches on her knees resting
back on her heels with her thighs wide open and her head slightly
tilted back. The night was almost over when they set out again and
at dawn they reached the prescribed place. Discouraged with their
faces ashen and some shrieking voices breaking through here and there
and clots of lava and startled locusts heaved into the air and everything
lay covered with murmuring vegetation and choked breathing and
you could hear the sun tearing loose like a shell from the rocks of
the sky the people at dawn's mercy *now! now!* Dr. Ineotis howled
enthusiastically and he meant the miracle and justice and the knife
grinder laughed aloud but the news had come. They would not die

Dr. Ineotis

easily as they had been told feeling nothing, but an indescribable or-
giastic death would put an end to their unjust and miserable lives.
Everything turned to marble. Before a hand could move or a knee
bend before fear could break the tight bands around their heads and
bellies and the place is filled with cries tears piss shit.

translated by Willis Barnstone

El Procurador   T. D. FRANGOPOULOS

"Damn it, I told him not to write that story!" Alonso thought sadly.

The literary circles of Anunciación had been shaken by the disappearance of the middle-aged poet Raul Mercader. The news, like all news in Boliguay since the time of the Benevolent Change, was unexpected—and the sequel, revealed publicly when the truth could no longer be suppressed, was even more shattering.

After years of insignificance the poet had succeeded in making a name for himself—six years after the pronunciamento carried out by the military Junta—when he signed, together with thirty-six other intellectuals, a statement demanding the re-establishment of freedom of the press in his country. That "Statement of the 37," as it was soon known in opposition circles, created a stir even abroad, having been published—in small print—by some liberal newspapers in Western Europe. In turn this publicity produced an impact all out of proportion to its intrinsic importance in the country where it was written, as is likely to happen in oppressed societies. All this gave Raul the status of an intellectual leader in the eyes of the Boliguayans, who had never bothered to read his books of poems, which, having come out in limited editions, were hard to find anyway.

Alonso was thinking of his last encounters with Mercader. It was at the time when some incorrigible romantics, clamoring for action

("subversive action," the regime of the Benevolent Change called it),
had made up their minds that Boliguayan intellectuals ought to do
something. There followed a number of meetings, half a dozen ideas
were put forward, and in the end it was decided to publish a review,
to which all intellectuals of the opposition would contribute something
recent. And not only intellectuals of Anunciación, but also a leading
figure like Emanuel Barraca of the second-largest city, Incarnación.

Nobody thought of asking Alonso to contribute; his literary output
consisted of only two poems written for a baker's daughter at the
time he was reading Law at the University, and both were execrable.
Besides, nowadays he was a successful lawyer with academic ambi-
tions—there was that chair of Comparative Law, vacant for so long—
and therefore it was highly improbable that he would have agreed
to appear as an intellectual of the Resistance even if he could. His
old friendship with Raul, however, and their daily contact, allowed
him to witness all the preparations for an enterprise, which was to
have such an unpleasant, one might even say tragic, outcome.

Raul, of course, had enthusiastically agreed to contribute to the review, but then he discovered that for six years he had hardly written
a thing: given his now greatly increased fame, it was not right to
measure him by the two epigrams he had circulated among his close
friends. The scarcely modest appellation "Simonideia" and the even
more ambitious pen name "Juvenal Victor Hugo" had appeared at
that time, which, depending on the listener's degree of kindness and
good manners, led him to tear his hair out or caused it to stand on
end.

"You understand," he told Alonso, "this time I need something of
high quality. It must be in accordance with the spirit of our deep
aversion for the Junta, yet not be too outspoken, lest we fall into the
hands of the Seguridad."

"Will it be a poem?" asked Alonso.

"Not necessarily," the poet answered generously. "I'm out of shape
after six years of not writing poetry, and my anger over this would
make me doubly bitter about the Government. It may be a piece of
prose."

"A short story?" Alonso inquired skeptically, knowing that his friend's talent for prose was praised only by malicious critics when they spoke of his poetry.

"Why not?" replied Raul Mercader. "I can write whatever I like, provided I transpose the plot into another time period."

"And you think that will protect you?"

"My dear Alonso, you musn't think I fear for myself," the poet said reprovingly. "I am only worrying about my family, and my friends who will publish the review."

Yes, pondered Alonso, no doubt Raul did not even have time to feel afraid before they caught him: from hints picked up here and there it was known that the Seguridad had a very efficient technique for arresting the people it wanted. After that, no one knew what would happen . . .

Anyway, Alonso was thinking, annoyed, I did warn him as soon as he told me his idea. Nobody could accuse him of not having expressed his misgivings as strongly as possible when, a few days later, he met Raul again at the latter's house.

"But are you insane?" he whispered, paling, when Raul finished reading him the first draft.

"Why?" asked the poet Mercader, looking obstinate. "As you see, I have set the story forty years ago, in the days of the dictatorship of Caromanos. Besides," he added quickly, "nobody will understand the allusion."

"What allusion, man? You are calling a spade a spade!"

"Not at all!" Raul shook his mane of hair. "To begin with, I describe the Prosecutor as a married man, whereas everybody knows that . . ."

"And was it necessary to add the detail that he had a famous collection of Inca pottery in his study? Nobody will be fooled; everyone will know what you mean!"

"All right," said Raul nonchalantly, "I can leave out that detail."

"And you think you'll still fool anybody?"

"My aim is not to fool, but to instruct!" the poet declared emphatically. "To teach intellectuals that it is their duty to take the lead in a crusade! And to do that, I must reveal—or at least put on record,

since everyone knows it anyway—the truth about the man who is
now Minister of Culture!"

"Not so loud, Raul, for God's sake! Walls have ears!"

"You're right," Raul replied a little more quietly, "it is only in
parks and public squares that one can talk freely nowadays. But what
kind of intellectuals are we if we don't . . ."

Alonso broke in with a hurried whisper:

"What I cannot understand is why you insist so much on the suspicious financial dealings of the . . . let us say, of the Prosecutor's
client. Do you believe anybody is interested in them any longer? I
mean, do you think there are still people in Boliguay who think he's
honest? Even if there are, he's doing his daily best to disillusion them.
You have only to read his declarations."

"I refuse to lower the level of my work by quoting excerpts from
his speeches!" said the poet with a hurt expression. "To begin with,
he is illiterate."

"I agree, his Spanish is unspeakable," said Alonso. "But what do
you expect them to learn at the Military College? Tirso de Molina
or Góngora? No," he continued, "I am not referring to the way he
murders our noble Castilian tongue, but to what he actually says.
He doesn't even try to conceal the fact that all his actions are planned
with the interests of the United Tomato Company in mind."

"All the more reason for bringing that old embezzlement charge
into the open!" Mercader replied warmly.

"Possibly, but in such a way as to be reasonably safe. Once again,
is it necessary to give so many details about the matter that even
little children will realize you are talking of a factual occurrence?
This naive transposition to another period won't help. Why must you
write, for instance, that when his regimental colonel found out about
the theft, he slapped him in the face in the presence of thirty witnesses
in the Military Mess?"

"But those were the things the Prosecutor knew!"

"Couldn't you omit all those details without weakening the plot?"

"Of course I could," Raul Mercader replied after some thought. "But
then my hints won't be clear enough."

"But that's exactly what you have to avoid, this exaggerated clarity.

It is also unnecessary, in my opinion, to refer to that incident with the wife of Captain Jiménez."

"All right, I can take that out as well. But don't ask me to omit the fact that he failed to be promoted because during the war with Uruvia, he managed to remain always at a safe distance from the front."

"If you breathe a word about that, you're doomed!" whispered Alonso. "You know how sensitive he is about his alleged military career!"

"But what will remain, then, of the story?" the poet asked plaintively. "A commonplace affair with a slight detective interest—the unexplained death of a well-known judicial bureaucrat."

"You might let it be understood, drop a hint, that the Prosecutor's death from heart disease—when it was known he was in perfect health—gave rise to suspicion because it occurred only one week after the pronunciamento," Alonso said. "But that's all. Not a word about the frequent calls of—of our character—on the Prosecutor. Not a word about his threat that soon he and his friends would be ruling Boliguay, and, above all, of course, not a word about the incident with the file."

"You mean to say the business with Zurbarán? But it's the most exciting, the crucial point in the whole story" said Raul astonished. "Besides," he added with moody self-satisfaction, "it's the best-written part."

"You're mad to think that today in Boliguay you can get away with publishing that a Minister—even in old times—got angry with a former Conservative politician and deported him because the politician asked the widow of a Prosecutor if, among a dead man's papers, there was a file on the inquiry concerning the Minister! I'm no longer speaking as your friend." Alonso continued, "but in my professional capacity as your lawyer. Damn it all, pull yourself together before it is too late!"

"But if I leave out the fact that there was such a file among the Prosecutor's papers, what remains of the story? And how do I explain that his death occasioned suspicious rumors? In that case he might as well have died a natural death. After all, thousands of people do suffer from heart diseases without knowing it. Will you let me write, at least, that shortly before he was found dead in his office, two mysterious strangers in long raincoats had called on him?"

"Of course not!"

"Nor that the Prosecutor had applied, immediately after the pronunciamento, for leave to travel abroad—for pleasure, he said?"

"Not even that."

"At least," the poet Mercader almost begged, "could I leave in the clue that, upon hearing the radio report that the military Junta had taken over, the Prosecutor looked anxious and murmured something that his wife took to be: "Caramba! He said he would do it and he did it, the dirty thief!""

"Nor that."

"Then I might leave in the paragraph where the Prosecutor instructs his secretary to say he's not there, locks himself in his office, and is overheard opening his safe and destroying documents. Then the reader will be prepared for what comes next."

"You could do something else," Alonso replied finally, exhausted by his friend's obstinate bargaining. "You could say, for instance, that the Prosecutor had heard his client bragging about the forthcoming pronunciamento, but didn't think it worth mentioning to anybody because he thought it was a naive attempt to intimidate him. That way, your story becomes true fiction, since we now know that the plan for the pronunciamento was both real and, as proved by success, very clever."

"I'd like to write it as I first conceived it," said Raul Mercader with plaintive obstinacy.

"Then I advise you not to publish it."

"But the others will think I'm scared."

"Write something else."

"There's no time, and I'm not in the mood. I looked again at the Simonideian epigrams. They aren't fit to be published, and I have nothing else."

"In that case," said Alonso, "write a story set in an unspecified country and a vague time. Copy Kafka, steal from Camus. Have a strange castle-owner recount, in the course of a gloomy gothic dinner-party, some improbable story about a confessor in the Middle Ages who knew a secret he didn't dare use, for instance, a conspiracy that couldn't help succeeding. But the kind of stuff you have been thinking about, man—prosecutors and so on, vanishing files with State secrets in them—forget it! Please remember the Benevolent Change we're living under: Boliguay Católico!"

But then, he wouldn't listen to me, Alonso reflected sadly as he recalled how they learned gradually about Raul Mercader's disappearance.

It was not hard to guess what had happened. Despite the warnings of his faithful friend, the poet insisted on submitting his manuscript for publication in the review. Alonso succeeded only in persuading him to show it to another lawyer, who suggested that the story be cut down to a third of its original length. Further cuts and changes, even regarding fundamental character traits, were made by the editor-in-chief. Finally, after a meeting that lasted many hours, the editorial board decided to reject even the truncated text. It was a fact that no one dared publish that sort of thing in the Boliguay of the Benevolent Change. Even the most outspoken writers of the opposition have a minimum self-preservation instinct. But with all that, the poet Don Raul Prieto de Mercader y Mercader vanished from Anunciación, and nobody knew where he had been taken.

The Seguridad of Boliguay was good at its job. Not all who pose as rebels and resistance heroes are necessarily what they seem to be. Even less so if they are intellectuals. And, as it emerged from the text of the story—which was subsequently lost without trace—Mercader knew too much. More than most Boliguayans. And that, the regime of the Benevolent Change could not forgive!

("There are such things as accidents," said the Minister of Culture, when asked by foreign correspondents how it happened that a corpse, which resembled Raul Mercader, was washed ashore on a beach. The fact that the corpse was in pajamas and bore black marks on his neck and on other parts of the body was not explained—not even in the official autopsy report, for the report was stamped *secret*.)

Alonso realized that he had discussed the contents of the story so much that he had almost forgotten its style and literary merit. He had even begun to feel confused about details. Was it Raul, for instance, or he himself who had suggested a scene in which the Prosecutor would try to dissuade the officer from looking upon Hitler's suicide as an exemplary ending for a military career? Still, it was just as well that he didn't remember clearly. Who knows what might happen if he showed signs of an accurate full memory!

One thing he did recall vividly was the title of the unfortunate Mercader's story: "El Procurador," the Prosecutor. (At a certain point, one of them—which?—had gone so far as to propose, jokingly, to camouflage the Prosecutor as a psychoanalyst, and they laughed at the idea of calling the story—in pidgin Spanish, of course—"El Psichenalidor" . . .)

One day, Alonso thought suddenly—while the mortal remains of Mercader, by virtue of the process of decomposition, were discarding the last visible signs of torture—one day *I* will write that story. When we are free. Certainly not before.

translated by Rodis Roufos

Weather-Change STRATIS TSIRKAS

Two girls were walking down Calle Almirante Pérez. In the wintry
light their black boots resounded in step along the pavement. The
city didn't show that many months before, suddenly in one night,
it had been stripped of freedom. The radio programs were cut off,
the telephones stopped working; then the guitars were locked up. No
more songs; the city went dumb. Deadly silence spread everywhere,
like a fall of black snow. Hour after hour the paving stones of Plaza
Simón Bolívar would be heard splitting slowly, two by two, under
the tank-treads: a horrid rattle like the cracking spine of a hanged
man.

There wasn't room for four abreast on the pavement. The two men
going up the hill with packages under their arms hesitated a moment.
The short, plump one was a priest. The other, well on in years, bony,
with his clothes worn out, stopped short and sighed. The girls separated,
walked around them both, and met again behind them without speaking. The tall man caught the brunette throwing him a quick glance.
In the chilly breeze a few strands of the blonde's hair floated against
the stubble on his face.

The priest said, "Sorry to be making you do all this work, Pepito."

"It's not that. I can't get used to them—the minis, I mean. Now
they've gone twelve inches above the knee."

The priest laughed cheerfully, his cheeks reddening. He was very young and only his clerical collar and black bib revealed his calling. Nobody knew exactly what was his connection with the Irish Embassy. Friends had seen him with the Ambassador's wife distributing parcels in the poor quarters.

Buses, cars, and taxis were passing them, pulling uphill and covering them with exhaust. Almirante Pérez had been made a one-way street now. This, and the silence of the young—the girls and boys who once used to come down arm in arm, discussing excitedly—was all that showed the change. Otherwise the same shops: a photographer's studio with ballerinas and generals in the window, yellow flowers pointed like spears in a flower shop, a boutique with a roll of fantastically expensive silk rolled out and a huge bottle of French perfume in the corner. Another boutique: a red blouse, red skirt on a rack, arms and legs stretched out like some crucified wax girl, who had burned up, leaving behind her unwrinkled clothes. An American surplus store, an antique shop, a cafeteria, a grocery store with a refrigerated window and steel shelves. In the doorway, in a spotless apron was the grocer.

"Eh, viejo!" he called to Pepito; but he was gazing at the priest, and with his middle finger stroking a grizzled moustache suggestively.

"Who's that? Does he know you?" the priest asked, uncomfortably.

"He came from over there too, along with the rest of us. He's the Dirty One, if you've ever heard of him. How many, thirty, years ago? We called him that after the fall of Madrid when we all came abroad. He gave in completely to despair, became a cynic, covered with lice. And he had loved a girl, dark, and skinny as a thrush. You should have seen her throw the Molotov cocktails—bull's-eye on the tank-turrets. And her love-making, he used to tell me, was red hot: so slow, so slow, the devil, she'd draw the very life out of him. But when the lightning hit, Madre de Dios, she'd open her mouth like a well and howl, 'Y no pasarán, y no pasarán!' and she'd grab her braids and stuff them in her mouth so nobody would hear, and she'd twitch like sardines on the sand . . . Y no pasarán! As if she was afraid they would, poor thing. Once he got over here he bought himself a cart and sold vegetables. He made quite a business of it. Gradually he pulled himself together, became a human being. But now, since the coup he's gone downhill again. Once more something inside has gone rotten."

They stopped at the crossing, waiting for the green light so they could cross over to where the grass of the square began. The priest muttered something hurriedly under his breath; he might have been praying for the grocer.

"Padre," Pepito interrupted, "is this the time to be saying paternosters! Come on, let's cross. For days now I've been wondering about you and asking What does he want of me, this, this papist? What if he was on the other side when all of us were bleeding to death for the Republic?"

"Are you crazy! Have you no sense of time? In 1936 I wasn't even born!"

"I don't mean you. Not you yourself. I mean your sort—a priest, a Catholic. How the hell did you and I ever get into the same hole? And here we are, the two of us, making a ladder now to help each other out into the light."

"Shall I tell you?"

"I know. The generals, the monopolies, the CIA."

"No. The suffering of Christ—that's what unites us."

"Could be. But that's an old tune."

They had arrived in front of the Catholic Youth Club. The doorman was standing behind the double-glass doors: an imposing type, one of the kind who immediately makes you feel inferior. Behind him, an ugly character in a black suit was pacing back and forth with a springy step. Neither one budged to open the door and help the priest and his companion, who by themselves put their parcels in the doorman's cubicle. The priest said, "Yes, these have to stay here; they're the projectors and reels for tonight's film, and don't let anyone touch them till I tell you." All this time the ugly one gazed indifferently at the ceiling.

"I don't like that one," said the priest once they had left.

"So," Pepito shrugged. "What do you expect? Security's already been notified about tonight."

"Did he recognize you?"

"What's to recognize?"

99

"Lucky you didn't open your mouth."

"What if I had?"

"Your Castilian accent. There aren't many of you here."

"The most they'd say would be: Father Sean O'Flaherty with his Spanish porter."

"No. They'd say Antonio Alomar, former political commissar of the 69th Division, with his little priest."

"That's bad. I didn't know you knew."

"Now you do."

"And who told you I might have changed my faith?"

"It's not you, Pepito. The times have changed. Shall we sit down somewhere and have a drink?"

"Better if we get away from here."

It was Antonio who was uneasy now. Plainclothesmen, scattered all over the place, were watching some toddlers crawling on the grass in their little overcoats. Old and new friends recognized him, astonished. What would they think? The two began to walk back down Almirante Pérez. The grocer, still in his doorway, pretended not to see them.

"What do you mean, Father, that times have changed?"

"Antonio Alomar, what do you take me for! Do you think I don't realize what's happening?" the priest said crossly. His arms jerked, palms open, and the little belly swelled under his black bib.

On the far pavement a retired civil servant in a scarf was offering his arm to his wife. Both wore thick glasses. They stopped and stared. Here, in the very midst of the New Moral Order, a priest quarreling with a tramp! Perhaps they should phone the police?

Again the priest blushed. He nudged Pepito's elbow to move on, and lowered his voice:

"That's not what I mean. You, all of us—white, yellow, and black—today, *today, I'm telling you*, we're all in the same boat! The same danger threatens us all!"

"So how do we fight it? With tape-recordings? By switching the soundtrack of a documentary, replacing the music with a speech?"

"A speech! Couldn't you recognize the words when we tested the film at the studio? It was Miguel de Unamuno at the University of

Salamanca. Right in front of the Fascist general, that half-mad cripple who shouted the slogan of the Moroccan Legion, 'Viva la muerte!' There he stood, the prophetic old man, just two steps from the grave, his voice cracked by the horror of the implacable tragedy, proclaiming his faith in life and in the spiritual values of mankind. Pepito, today the Word must begin to be heard again to put iron back in men's souls."

"With talk? With oblique references? Today, Father, if you don't call things by their real names, if you don't point straight at them, then anything you say, and however beautifully you say it, is water over the dam of tyranny. 'Look, see for yourselves,' they'll say, 'Who says there's no freedom?' "

"You very much underestimate the intelligence of the people. You, Antonio Alomar."

"Which people? What do you know about what's happening and what people are saying?"

"I do know, Pepito. Hilda Gómez died insane because, the day before, she saw her husband killed by torture and then her four-month-old baby dying the same way. Listen, Sister Carmen Borges Silveira is speaking to me: 'Father, they forced me to undress in front of my torturers and then they stuck electrodes inside my genital organs.' Conchita Maria Cocencia Avelar said: "They hung me on a pole by the knees and elbows and in this position gave me electric shocks with a 90-volt field telephone. In this position Sergeant Leo Hernando beat me with his club on the behind, the shins, the soles of my feet. Sometimes he'd stop hitting and begin sexual activity. My body was fondled and kissed and abused in such a way that I don't dare describe it to you for fear that your own soul, Father, might be damned.' "

They had stopped for five minutes or so, standing on the pavement at the beginning of Almirante Pérez. Meanwhile, the weather had changed, was overcast, but hot and thundering. As long as he was talking, the priest's face had shone. A shudder convulsed Antonio's bony shoulders. Sweat (or tears?) trickled, a very fine stream, through his unshaven beard. He started to speak and a lump in his throat hoarsened his voice. He broke out furiously:

"Amateurs! You're all amateurs! With films and a lot of talk you think you can . . . Naive, unsuspecting, ignorant! Just one example:

How could you trust me all alone in the studio to pack up your reels and projectors? What if I put a bomb in there too?"

"I know what you are. You'd never want innocent people killed."

"Not tonight, but right now! That ugly character, and the other one, the doorman."

"Even they're not to blame. They know not what they do."

Then came the crash of an explosion.

"Pepito?"

The priest started, and stretched out a hand, which was trembling.

The other was looking at him with an ambiguous smile. Then he said, "Don't worry. Just the blasting in Plaza Bolívar. They're pulling out the old tiles for the new marble paving."

translated by Kevin Andrews

The Target MANOLIS ANAGNOSTAKIS

The point is, what do you say *now?*
We've eaten well, drunk well,
carried our life quite well so far,
balancing small losses against small gains.
The point is, what do you say *now?*

Manolis Anagnostakis

1   POETICS

—You're betraying Poetry again, you'll say,
the most sacred expression Man has,
using it again as a means,
pack mule to your dark pursuits,
knowing full well the damage your example
will inflict on the young.

—Just tell me what *you* have not betrayed,
you and those like you, years on end,
selling off your belongings one by one
in international markets and common bazaars,
left now without eyes to see, ears to hear,
and lips sealed so you can't talk.
What sacred human expression are you preaching about?

I know: sermons and speeches again, you'll say.
All right, yes then! Sermons and speeches.

Words ought to be hammered in like *nails*.

So the wind won't take them away.

The Target

My child never liked fairy tales

yet they told him about Dragons and the faithful dog,
about Sleeping Beauty's travels and about the wild wolf,

but the child never did like fairy tales.

Now, in the evenings, I sit and talk to him,
I call the dog dog, the wolf wolf, the darkness darkness,
I point out the bad people with my hand, I teach him
names like prayers, I sing to him about our dead.

Oh, it's enough! We have to tell children the truth.

Manolis Anagnostakis

3   THE SKY

First let me take your hands,
let me feel your pulse,
then let's go together to the forest
and embrace the big trees
on whose every trunk we carved
the sacred names years ago,
let's spell them out together,
let's count them one by one
with our eyes turned to the sky as though in prayer.

The sky doesn't hide our particular forest.

Woodcutters don't come by here.

4 THESSALONIKI, DAYS OF A.D. 1969

On Egypt Street—first side-street on the right—
the Exchange Bank Building rises now,
tourist offices and emigration agencies.
And the kids can't play there any longer so much traffic goes by.
Besides, the kids have grown up, the days you knew are gone.
Now they don't laugh any more, don't whisper secrets, don't con-
    fide in each other,
those who have survived, I mean, because serious illness has taken
    its toll since then,
floods, ships sinking, earthquakes, armored soldiers,
they remember their fathers' words: you'll know better days.
It doesn't matter in the end if they never knew better days, they'll
    repeat the same lesson to their own children,
hoping always that the chain will break some day,
maybe with their children's children or their children's children's
    children.
For the time being, on the old street we mentioned, the Exchange
    Bank rises
—I exchange, you exchange, he exchanges—
tourist offices and emigration agencies
—we emigrate, you emigrate, they emigrate—
wherever I travel, Greece wounds me, said the Poet:
Greece of the beautiful islands, beautiful offices, beautiful
    churches,

Greece of the Greeks.

Manolis Anagnostakis

5   EPITAPH

You died—and then you too became: that good,
that brilliant man, head of a family, patriot.
Thirty-six wreaths went with you, three eulogies by
    vice-presidents,
seven decrees honoring the splendid services you rendered.

Oh, friend Lavrenti, I who alone knew what kind of dirt you
    were,
what fake currency, your whole life lived in a lie,
rest in peace, I won't come to disturb your quiet
(I'll redeem a whole life in silence,
at great expense, not at the price of your poor hide).
Rest in peace. As you always were in life: that good,
that brilliant man, head of a family, patriot.

You won't be the first nor indeed the last.

The Target

6   THE DECISION

Are you for or against?
Either way, answer with a yes or a no.
You've thought the problem over,
I'm sure it's given you trouble,
most things in life are troublesome:
children, women, insects,
noxious plants, wasted hours,
difficult passions, rotten teeth,
mediocre movies. And this will have troubled you for sure.
Speak responsibly then. Even if just a yes or no.
The decision is yours.
Of course we don't ask that you stop
your activities, interrupt your life,
your favorite newspapers, discussions
at the barber shop, your Sundays at the stadium.
One word only. Go ahead then:
are you for or against?
Think it over carefully. I'll be waiting.

Manolis Anagnostakis

Sunday. Lord, we thank you.
Receive us into your embrace like lost sheep.
We have sinned greatly, Lord, we have been very unjust.
Like unbelievers, we mourn for our worldly goods.
We have forgotten the eternal Spring of Paradise.
In your House we beseech you to forgive us.
This being Sunday we remember your commandments.
Do not abandon us, O Lord, to the darkness of the abyss.

(Besides, very recently, under instructions
from those in charge, we offered
our small contribution toward the reconstruction of your Sacred
  Temple.)

9   YOUNG MEN OF SIDON, 1970

Actually we shouldn't have any complaints.
Your company is good and warm-hearted, full of youth,
fresh young girls, sound-limbed boys,
full of passion and a love of life and action.
Your songs are good too, full of meaning and substance,
very, so very human, so moving,
about children dying on another continent,
about heroes killed in former years,
about revolutionaries Black, Green, or Yellowing,
about the sorrow of generally suffering Man.
You are to be commended especially for sharing
in uncertainties and for bringing to the struggles of our time
an immediate and active presence.
After this, I think you have every right
to play, to love, by twos, by threes,
and to let yourselves go, for God's sake, after so much exertion.

(They've made us grow old before our time, George, do you realize
    it?)

Manolis Anagnostakis

If—I say if . . .
If everything hadn't happened so early:
your expulsion from High School in the 11th grade,
then Haidari, St. Stratis, Makronisos, Idzedin.
If, at the age of 42, you hadn't contracted spinal arthritis
after those twenty years in prison,
with two cancellations on your back, a statement
of renunciation, when they isolated you in the Psychiatric Ward,
if—now an accountant in a grocery store—
no use to anyone any longer, a squeezed-out lemon,
a closed case, with ideas long outdated.
If—I say if . . .
with a little good will everything had happened somehow
    differently,
or through a chance occurrence, as happens to so many
classmates, friends, companions—I don't mean with no trouble
    at all,
but if . . .

(Enough. This isn't the stuff poems are made of. Don't insist.
Poems need a different mood to please, a different substance.

We've gone too heavy on the theme writing.)

12 SENTIMENTAL STORY   For Kosta Kouloufako

His father used to tell him: "You're not the one who's going to
    change the Greek way."
For a time he too believed, a child almost, that he could change it
(thirty years ago now, old years, who remembers them . . .).
But the practical example was set by his older brother,
he too a one-time savior apparent, very soon sobered up,
or rather brought to his senses prematurely, later private secretary
    to a minister
in a productive ministry with a large circle of private business
    clients.
And he, faithful son and brother, thought and thought,
saw the mistakes, diagnosed betrayals, weighed the pros and cons,
ended up talking about crimes committed and foreign intervention.
Besides, things had started getting more or less tight—
always bright in the head, it didn't take him long to choose.
Not of course that Mike would have actually saved the Greeks
    back then.
After all, they weren't saved by So-and-so or So-and-so . . . let's
    not mention names.
But, for God's sake, how can I put it, once upon a time we drank
    wine together,
hid in Arrianou Street chased by the fuzz,
kissed the same girls, exchanged passwords
(a very cheap story all this, sentimental, as though I didn't know
    it,
and life needs toughness—you're telling me—and "realism" above
    all).

And *now:*

You inside again and Mike outside again
(putting it rather grossly)—he a more important factor in the
    current situation,

as, let's admit it, in every situation so far.
You should become Greek, he says, get wise, become useful
to society for once, work for this unfortunate country of ours,
and he gives you advice in the name of old friendship and of
    "remember the time . . . ."

(I insist on telling—my language indeed raw—things that all
    of you know,
things I've said again and again and that others before me have
    said much better than me,
boring things that do not hold your interest any more,
like Sharon Tate's murder, for example, or Jackie's wedding, or
    the Kelvinator refrigerator.)

The Target

. . . And, basically, the extensions are missing,
that charming vagueness which suggests
second levels and unexpected perspectives,
which poses questions of interpretation, stimulates debate,
indicates structures, uncovers essences.
The purity of expression is missing, the *something else,*
finally, the prismatic quality of things—one would think
you have a hammer in your hand and like the gypsies
keep pounding incessantly on the same anvil.

—Like the gypsies
         we keep pounding
                incessantly
                      on the same anvil.

Manolis Anagnostakis

14 EPILOGUE (FRAGMENT)

And no self-delusions above all.

At most consider them as two dim floodlights in the fog,

as a postcard to absent friends with the single message: I live.

"Because," as my friend Tito rightly said once,
"No verse today will mobilize the masses,
No verse today will overthrow regimes."

So be it.
Disabled, show your hands. Judge so that you may be judged.

translated by Edmund and Mary Keeley

Arrogance and Intoxication

The Poet and History in Cavafy

D. N. MARONITIS

To Six Friends

In times like ours, when history is produced and written by machines with human appendages, of what use can the poet's voice be?

In a small, poor country like ours, where land, seas, and men are transformed by the electronic computers of the powerful into programs of war, economic, and tourist policies, what can be salvaged by the few words selected by the poet's diffused senses?

In such a critical time as that of our land today, when the daily word is paid for dearly, why should the poet's voice make his and our guilty survival official?

I ask these three naive questions not to stimulate the superficial anxiety of the pseudo-sensitive, nor to indicate the way to resolve meta-physical lassitude, but in order to define the three kinds of prisons in which people of our century live, whether they understand it or not.

The first prison still has many comforts; its wounds are so well-decorated that it is hard to distinguish the howl from profiteering and

* Material in square brackets has been added by the translator.

advertising. The second trap is more familiar, since we have been in it for several years. Our present cell, however, is of the third kind: in it we live our own and other people's history, in it we keep vigil and wish for clean air and water.

Still, some people, with open eyes and sober mind, have shouted, and are still shouting, that it is very easy to pass from the first to the second prison, and from the second to the third. As they saw the space around them narrowing and closing, they quite early began to use a symbolic warning language, the prisoners' language. They knocked at closed doors, they wrote signal dates on the wall, they tested their biological reflexes: whether the sun still provides them with its driblets of optimism, whether the night does not paralyze their mind with its motorized nightmares, whether their dreams retain their sharp and threatening meaning, whether their memory is still pensive and hard, dwelling on whatever good or evil was said and done by our dead and our living. They asked and keep asking who are they who think they have the right to grab their daily food, sleep, and love in the name of history, of the ghosts of the past, or of the visions of the future.

And the poet? It depends on the kind of prison he is in; on whether his land had trained him in the symbolic language of prisoners; on whether he himself had the sincerity, the courage, and the art to carry that language even further and deeper; on whether his biological reflexes functioned well.

In our own land there has been no dearth of poets. It is the job of our poetry's scholars to study whether and how this symbolic language has grown and how far it has reached inside modern Greek poetry. In this essay, we shall dwell on a single poet, dead forty years, who knew that language well and practiced it correctly. I am referring to Constantine Cavafy, the Alexandrian, and, more specifically to one poem of his: "Darius," one of the best known and most timely these days. It is a portrait fashioned around 1920 which narrates in tragicomic tone the poet's confusion as he is caught in the hooks of history. A poet in a cage, and the cage caught in a net; the poet a prisoner of his poetic idea, at the moment Roman legionnaires are preparing to catch him as well as his country in their net. An old-fashioned person would have given that portrait the title, "The Poet and History." For us, too, this title is convenient. Yet, before going into our main topic, we must provide a few explanations to assure better communication.

Usually, when we speak of history, we think of it as dealing with the past, and see there its beginning or even its end. Actually, the reverse is true: history begins with today and moves toward tomorrow. We only link it with the past to derive help from the experience of others in fashioning our own fate, today and tomorrow, and not idly to contemplate and forget ourselves in what our ancient ancestors did. Some might say that if history is brought into the present, it risks becoming identified with current journalistic events. No. A clear and well-trained mind dwells on those events of the present which, by their magnitude and significance, will feed tomorrow's historical science. We would not dare call history our own loves, our marriage, or even our own physical death. But war or refugee migration, occupation or slavery, famine and mass death, violence and lack of freedom, these we call history, and rightly so. When we refer then to the poet's—or anyone's—historical consciousness, we mean his reaction to the deep wounds of our collective life, to those great waves which you cannot avoid even if you want to, even if you are a coward or a traitor.

The poet's historical consciousness is judged therefore by this common measure, which applies to everyone else, and by a second criterion: how and to what degree the critical historical event of the present is absorbed, transformed, and projected in the poetic work. The poet's political activity is the biographer's and the historian's domain. (His private life is nobody's concern, although recently it has become fashionable for psychologists and scandalmongers to deal with it, too.) The literary critic's task lies principally in the crystallized poetic work, which can be seen in two ways: either totally severed from the umbilical cord joining it to the poet, or in its immediate relation to its creator. I do not know which is best. The first way appears to me simpler and more natural, although affording greater probability for misunderstandings. The second, for those who have the means and time to follow it, appears more certain and more scientific, but leads, sooner or later, into a poetry that needs the crutches of critical interpretation, a poetry for the few and chosen. Our present topic however is more concrete: when we interpret a poem we should not forget that a good poem contains in itself the elements necessary to judge whether there is a gap between the poet's life and his writing, or whether they are consistent, and to what degree. Knowledge of the poet's life and activity does not alter this reality.

The reader may well wonder exactly why I chose Cavafy's "Darius." I would reply: because I believe that this poem takes the bull by the horns, and provides a very clear and wise answer to our question about the relation between the poet and the critical historical events of his time and place. Of course, there are other answers as well in modern Greek poetry: Dionysius Solomos' answer, for instance (especially in the last, "antipoetic," part of his "Hymn to Liberty"), appears to lie at the antipodes of Cavafy's; on the other hand, George Seferis' poetry, with the "Old Man at the Riverside" as its main signal, defines a third position, differing from the preceding two; finally, Odysseas Elytis' apologetic attitude toward the same problem, which appears most clearly in *Axion Esti*, is of equal interest. I should confess that my initial intention was to define and comment on all four positions, the one next to the other; but this would carry my study too far and require a book to do it. I limited myself, therefore, to Cavafy's "Darius," which, I believe, remains, fifty years after its composition, a good and clear mirror where all of us—including our poets—can see our reflection. It may be that the image the mirror offers is not very comforting, but on the other hand it is truthful, even today—and that is important.

Lastly, I would like to explain my concern in this study with well-known and established names of our poetry—do I lack the courage to judge younger and more contemporary voices? In this instance, we need poems that do not deliberately belong to "engaged" poetry, so as not to come up against just or unjust prejudices; moreover, we need poems whose identity is known and easily perceived by all; finally, our very recent poetry cannot be deciphered without violent and hasty gestures, and it is useful to avoid these here. And now to Cavafy and his "Darius."

Cavafy's historical consciousness can be subject to several interpretations. Not a few believe, and have maintained in their writings, that Cavafy's historicism (and, by extension, his symbolism) constitutes a conscious means of concealment, a fabricated alibi for the poet, to cover up personal wounds and, more concretely, his unorthodox sexuality. The leader of this psychoanalytical interpretation is Timos Malanos, who has devoted much time and effort to the Alexandrian poet's work, trying to interpret a poetry which at bottom repelled and scandalized him. Cavafy's concern with history was perceived more profoundly and more carefully by some recent students, Greek as well as foreign. According to them, history, in its daily flow or in its scholarly crystallization, constitutes the hinterland of Cavafy's poetry, the fertile soil in which the poet deposits his personal experiences and his individual feelings (not exclusively the sexual ones), awaiting later, sometimes for long years, the outcome of that sowing; if the plant that finally sprouts satisfies him, he embalms it in a poem—otherwise he buries it again. In addition to these somewhat general and vague comments, I should like to refer the reader more concretely to three interpretations given. Each illuminates Cavafy's historicism from a different angle; all three together show clearly the meaning, function, and high degree of sensitivity of the poet's historical consciousness.

The first interpretation is that of C. M. Bowra; it is found in an otherwise rather mediocre essay devoted to the Alexandrian poet.* I detach and quote here one paragraph which touches on a very important problem of the literature of our century, within the framework of which Bowra places Cavafy's historicism.

The poet needs symbols and myths to give individual form to his indeterminate thoughts. If he shrinks, as he well may, from abstractions because they are too vague and in the end too false, he must have symbols to convey his meaning in its fullness. This has not always been a serious problem. The ancient Greek poets had in their incomparable mythology images and symbols for any situation. Dante had hardly less in the coherent theology of mediaeval Christianity: even the Renaissance and the

* [C. M. Bowra, "Constantine Cavafy and the Greek Past," *The Creative Experiment* (London, 1949), pp. 32–33; Greek version, p. 227, in] *Anglo-Hellenic Review*, IV, 225–237.

eighteenth century had in their revived classical myths something which
served many useful purposes. But the modern world has no such coherent
and recognized system. When Mallarmé set out to compose an entirely
symbolical poetry, he found his symbols in his own experience, with the
result that many of his readers are unable to catch his full meaning or his
exact intonations. Other poets have seen the difficulty and tried to meet it
by creating or adopting coherent mythologies. What Yeats found for a
time in old Irish legends, what Eliot found for *The Waste Land* in figures
and events from anthropology, Cavafy found much less laboriously in the
Hellenistic past.

This is Bowra's interpretation; it indicates, although somewhat flabbily,
the beginnings of Cavafy's historicism or better, of his mythology.

George Seferis has given the second interpretation in an essay entitled "C. P. Cavafy, T. S. Eliot: Parallels." Commenting on Eliot's
famous phrase concerning the "objective correlative," which a poet
must seek in his work, he adds:

What Eliot is saying I imagine, is that in order to be able to express his
emotion the poet has to find a setting of situations, a framework of events,
a form-type, which will be like the sights of a rifle; when the senses are
"sighted" in this way they will find themselves directed at the particular
emotion. The framework of events in the *Odyssey*, the *Divine Comedy*, or
Antony and Cleopatra, for example (and I mean not only the plot of these
works, but also, and mainly, the psychology and pattern of behavior of
their characters) is the "objective correlative" of the special emotion which
Homer, Dante, or Shakespeare wish to express; the objective correlative is
a tool of accuracy.

Cavafy seems to be constantly using this method; and as the years pass,
he seems to reject altogether the unframed expression of emotion.*

I would like to continue this quotation to make Seferis' interpretation
even clearer but the phrase quoted adequately explains that Cavafy's
historicism was not a mere cloak for psychological inadequacy. And
so I move to the third interpretation.

This is provided by Stratis Tsirkas in his large and valuable book

---

* First published in the *Anglo-Hellenic Review* (vol. III), later incorporated in his
Essays [Translated as, "Cavafy and Eliot—A Comparison," in George Seferis, *On the
Greek Style. Selected Essays in Poetry and Hellenism*, translated by Rex Warner
and T. D. Frangopoulos (Boston and Toronto, 1966); quoted passage, p. 145.]

on *Cavafy and His Times* (Athens, 1958). One may object to many
points in this book, yet its importance is great, because it shows, not
generally and vaguely but on unshakable evidence, how unself-centered
was Cavafy's poetry (at least until 1911), how closely tied it was
to concrete events of the period and of the poet's city, how the historical
dimension of his work is born, and how it takes form. Somewhere
in the middle of his book, a little before examining the poem *Expecting
the Barbarians*, in a methodological chapter entitled "The Three Keys"
(pp. 315–320), Tsirkas defines those three keys as follows:

> The basic motif, at least in Cavafy's moralistic poems, is of course given
> by the contemporary real event. We shall call this the second key or the
> second source. The first key, which in its intensity covers the second, is
> the literary source, the historical event. The third key is still lower; only
> the trained ear can still hear it. This key suggests, it does not declare;
> precisely because of this its effect is slower but also more persistent. Its
> source lies in the poet's experiences, in the psychical event. (p. 318)

Naturally the term "key" is used here in its musicological sense.
A little later, Tsirkas uses an image to describe the way the three
keys function simultaneously in Cavafy's poetry.

> The harmonic correspondence of the three keys provides depth to
> Cavafy's poem. Depth in time; depth in vision; depth in thought; depth in
> emotion. The first two keys (the concrete incident and the literary source)
> operate like two mirrors facing one another: they create the sense of an
> endless perspective. Between the two mirrors the poet raises his lamp, his
> psychical ego. Its most minute movement reveals new worlds, still deeper,
> even more distant. Nevertheless, all these efforts toward the ideal goal
> never break down the consciousness of reality. This multiplication of the
> ego, while giving the impression of a great crowd behind the subject, offers
> at the same time the confirmation of its real presence in countless facsimiles.
> (p. 320)

Finally, I add a fourth interpretation, the poet's own; after the preceding three we can perceive its true meaning. In the last years of
his life, Cavafy used to say: "I am a historical poet; I could never
write a novel or a play; but I feel inside me a hundred and twenty-five
voices telling me that I could write history." What kind of history?
The reading of "Darius" will show.

D. N. Maronitis

Darius*

Phernazis the poet is at work
on the important part of his epic:
how Darius, son of Hystaspes,
took over the Persian kingdom.
(It's from him, Darius, that our glorious king,
Mithridates, Dionysus and Eupartor, descends.)†
But this calls for serious thought; he has to analyze
the feelings Darius must have had:
arrogance, maybe, and intoxication? But no—more likely
a certain insight into the vanities of greatness.
The poet ponders the matter deeply.

But his servant, running in,
cuts him short to announce very important news.
The war with the Romans has begun.
Most of our army has crossed the borders.

The poet is dumbfounded. What a disaster!
How can our glorious king,
Mithridates, Dionysus and Eupator,
bother about Greek poems now?
In the middle of a war—just think, Greek poems!

Phernazis gets worked up. What a bad break!
Just when he was sure to distinguish himself
with his *Darius*, sure to make
his envious critics shut up once and for all.
What a postponement, terrible postponement of his plans.

And if it's only a postponement, that would be fine.
But are we really safe in Amisus?

---

* Translation by Edmund Keeley and Philip Sherrard; from *C. P. Cavafy: Selected Poems* (Princeton University Press, in press).
† Mithridates VI, Eupator Dionysus (the "Great"), King of Pontus from 120 to 63 B.C., was the last of a line ruling under the same name.

The town isn't very well fortified,
and the Romans are the most awful enemies.
Are we, Cappadocians, really a match for them?
Is it conceivable?
Are we to compete with the legions?
Great gods, protectors of Asia, help us.

But through all his distress and agitation
the poetic idea comes and goes insistently:
arrogance and intoxication—that's the most likely, of course:
arrogance and intoxication is what Darius must have felt.

Perhaps it is enough just to listen to the poem, once or several times.
If we do not limit ourselves to that, letting the poem approach us
by its own autonomous movement, if we seek instead the assistance
of the biographer, the historian, and the philologist, then, I fear, our
misfortune and confusion will be no less than those of the poet
Phernazis. For almost all the tools needed to put into effect Tsirkas'
three keys are missing: namely:

(a) We know nothing concerning the network of concrete events
on which the poet exercised this particular poetic phantasy (Tsirkas'
second key).

(b) Nor is the literary source of the poem determined, so that its
careful reading and comparison to Cavafy's text may show its place
and its function in the poem (Tsirkas' first key).

(c) Finally, while in some other poems of Cavafy's the psychical
event (Tsirkas' third key) can be perceived through certain signal
words of the poem or even through its omissions, "Darius" is a completely enclosed stage set, letting no whisper—or hardly any—from
behind the scenes reach our ears.

To these essential deficiencies, a "pedantic" philologist might add
a few more: in studying the form of the poem and trying, through
its chinks, to perceive the hidden substance, he would seek at least
three kinds of critical studies, which are in fact missing from the otherwise rich bibliography on Cavafy. More concretely:

(a) There is no chart in which the poems are classified according to their linguistic form. Let me explain. "Darius" is written in a third-person objective narration; but how many and which other poems by Cavafy follow this particular form? Furthermore, how many and which project the first-person singular, whether authentic or fictional? For instance, "The Walls" is composed in an authentic first-person, whereas the "Melancholy of Jason Cleander" refracts, by its title, the first-person singular into a third person. Another series of poems shows a preference for the second-person singular. Why and to what extent does this happen in Cavafy's poetry? Finally, one would wish to know which of his poems use a genuine first-person plural (as in the "Interruption") and which use it as an alibi (whether in the verb or in the use of the pronoun "our"), thus rendering, in ambiguous fashion, the poet and the reader accomplices in the poem's *mise en scène*. This is the case, for instance, in "Herodes Atticus," in the line, "Alexander from Seleuceia, one of *our* good sophists," or in the lines of "Darius," "from him . . . our glorious king . . . descends."

(b) Also lacking in the bibliography on Cavafy is a study which would investigate carefully the use and meaning of the word "poet" in his poems. A hasty glance shows that Cavafy attributes this title with great care to himself and to some of his fictional personages. In most cases, however, he uses synonomous or related words, located nearer or farther away from the word "poet," but in no case exact substitutes for it: technician, artisan, artist, sculptor; and, further, sophist, grammarian, orator, scholar, and so on.

(c) Finally, in order to assess the character of the poet Phernazis, we would need a study of the professional artist's role in Cavafy's poetry; as in the case of the subjects of such poems as "Dionysus' Escort," "Sculptor from Tyaneia," and "Philhellene."

I stop listing omissions because the reader might rightly accuse me of "arrogance and intoxication"; still, what I am asking for are the tools necessary in any research that aspires to avoid improvisation. Let us see now what we do have: I. The poem itself; II. The date of its composition (1920); III. Historical sources referring to Mithridates and his wars with the Romans, or to King Darius and the events, in history and anecdote, which brought him to the throne. I begin in reverse order, from end to beginning.

III. *The historical framework*. With the exception of the poet, Phernazis, who both as a name and as a person appears to have been pure invention on the part of Cavafy, the other persons, events, and things in the poem (Darius, Mithridates and his wars with the Romans, the Cappadocians and Amisus) are authentic elements of history.

Concerning Darius, the Persian king (522–486 B.C.), who founded a new royal dynasty by replacing the last descendant of the dynasty of Cyrus through conspiracy, I refer to Herodotus (III, 61–81).

Concerning Mithridates VI, Eupator (126–63 B.C.), the Hellenized king of Pontus, who fought the Romans in the East with persistence and initially not without success, there are many references in ancient and later historical sources. They mention his strategic ability (never impeded, apparently, by moral principle), his linguistic ability, and his habituation to poison (the latter made it necessary for him, when at the last moment he wanted to kill himself, to resort to the sword of a Celtic mercenary—poisons could not affect him any more). The main sources are Appian's *Roman History* (book XII) and Plutarch's *Pompey*. These sources describe in detail the three wars associated with his name (86–63 B.C.), whose protagonists were, on the Roman side, Sulla, Murena, and Pompey, and on Mithridates' side, himself, Archelaus, and others. In addition to Plutarch and Appian, we find information on Mithridates, his activities, and his tragic end, in Strabo, Cicero, Diodorus, Dio Cassius, Athenaeus, and other later authors.

It is not easy to determine the exact fictional date of the poem; if we take line 14 literally, then we must be at the beginning of the First Mithridatic War, at the time of Sulla's campaign (86 B.C.). George Savvidis speculates that the fictional date of the poem is 74 B.C., that is, during the Second Mithridatic War, when the battle scene moved from mainland Greece to Asia Minor and the Pontus. I suppose that Savvidis was led to his guess by line 15, which is ambiguous, and by the fact that the poem needs a more dramatic moment for Cappadocia than that which 86 B.C. would provide. For the poem itself, the matter is of no particular significance. As for Amisus, we know that it fell to the Romans in 71 B.C.

A more substantive question concerns the concrete historical source or sources which Cavafy utilized in staging the historical framework of "Darius." This is not an easy topic and requires systematic research. From a hasty comparison of the ancient sources and Cavafy's text, I am led to the supposition that Cavafy knew, directly or indirectly, the relevant narration of Appian. My hypothesis is based mainly on two details of expression which bring Cavafy's "Darius" close to Appian's narration. One is Mithridates' titles, "Dionysus and Eupator"; we can read both together in Appian: "And he was succeeded by his son, Mithridates, whose names were Dionysus and Eupator" (XII, 2, 10). The second, more indicative detail relates to Mithridates' descent from Darius. We read in Appian (XII, 16, 112): "And Mithridates died, being the eleventh descendant from Darius, son of Hystaspes, of the Persians." This detail I did not find anywhere except in Appian; however, because I did not investigate all secondary sources, my hypothesis may well be proven totally unfounded.

The name of the fictional Phernazis, which Savvidis considers Persian, cannot be found in Pâpe's dictionary. Did Cavafy invent this too? Or did he know it from another source, a non-Greek one? If the former were true, then the only name which sounds similar to that of Phernazis and which has some relation to Mithridates is Pharnaces; this was the name of Mithridates' son, the one who betrayed him to Pompey. Is Cavafy playing with this name? Perhaps.

II. *Historical background.* The date of composition, or only of publication, of "Darius" is, as we said, 1920. What was happening in Alexandria at that time that stimulated Cavafy to write "Darius"? Unfortunately Tsirkas' valuable study, which relates historical events in Alexandria, and more generally in Egypt, with concrete poems by Cavafy, stops at 1911. Indeed Tsirkas appears to believe that from 1911 on, after the British occupation, Cavafy was disillusioned with the Greek community's affairs, and ceased his poetic dialogue with his city's historical background. I do not know if he is right. Personally, in many of Cavafy's poems written after 1911 I feel a historical pulse which cannot be explained if Tsirkas' hypothesis were admitted. Let us hope that Tsirkas will continue his research into the more mature poems of Cavafy, thus the echoes of Alexandrian history will become clearer and more concrete in the poet's later production as well. For the time being, since we have no help on this point, we have nothing more specific to base "Darius" on than the political wartime confusion which dominated the Balkans in 1920.

I. *The poem.* We shall start with certain observations concerning morphology, in the hope that this is the safest way to approach the poem's substance. First, punctuation.

1. Naturally I have not changed the punctuation of the poem.* However, when a researcher is dealing with as characteristic a lack of orthodoxy in punctuation as that of Cavafy, his duty does not stop there. There is no doubt that punctuation in Cavafy is less syntactic (that is to say, it is concerned less with logical sequence) and more phonetic (it suggests, that is, to the person who will read, or better will recite, the poem a wholly binding manner for the expression of the poetic word). Through his punctuation the poet stages a scene; he does not allow the actor any arbitrary gesture. I am referring here not only to his famous dashes or parentheses but even to the manner in which he places a comma or a period. To attempt an analytical assessment of the punctuation of the entire poem would take us too far. I will mention only two examples to justify the emphasis I put on these general considerations. The first example concerns the comma or rather the two commas which [in the Greek text] isolate the adjective "envious" from the substantive preceding it, "critics," and the adverbial phrase that follows it, "once and for all" [line 24 in the translation]. The second example relates to the unexpected period after the word "confound" [in the translation the effect described occurs with the period after "all"]. It emphasizes the content of lines 22–24 by turning into a main sentence what we had expected to be subordinate. This is not merely a matter of keeping the reader's voice in suspense; if the poet wanted to achieve that, he would have used suspension points. What occurs is a sudden lowering of the voice, a complete stop, prior to our hearing the exclamatory sentence of line 25.

2. "Darius," as we have already stressed, is syntactically organized in a third-person narration. The poet is narrator and commentator

---

* It is altered in the translation.

as is shown clearly by lines 1–4, 11, 13–14, 16, 21, and 34–35 (on line 16 the poet's voice stops at "dumbfounded," and on line 21 before the words "What a bad break"). But what exactly is happening in the rest of the poem? For instance, who speaks the lines within the first parenthesis? The poet? Phernazis? Or is there a third, invisible prompter? And how should we hear lines 14–15, without the quotation marks which would have allowed us to attribute them directly to a messenger? Who is the intermediary? The poet? Or Phernazis? And especially in lines 16–33 (without quotation marks, either), who gathers and communicates to us these confessed and unconfessed thoughts of Phernazis? Finally, who deciphers the last thought of Phernazis at the poem's climax? There is no doubt, I think, that, as a whole, the poem functions theatrically. Cavafy is the stage director and in part the actor; we are the audience, and at times his coactors; Phernazis himself—with the visions of his inspiration at the start, with the echo of the war's announcement in his ears afterward, and again alone at the end, until the conclusion—grimaces more than he speaks; he acts out a kind of pantomine while his words and thoughts reach us through the interposition of a prompter, who is not always and necessarily to be identified with the poet. Several students of Cavafy have said that in the technique of his poems the poet follows the teachings of the Alexandrian mimes of Herondas. Perhaps they are not wrong.

3. That morphological observation may help us pass to a more substantive question. It was Seferis, I believe, who first compared Cavafy to the sea-demon of the Odyssey, old Proteus, who changed forms, one after the other, in order not to betray his secrets and his identity. To tame him and to get from him certain, rather unpleasant, information, Menelaus needed the help of Proteus' daughter, Eidothea. Seferis' comparison goes straight to the point: Cavafy, like Proteus, does not give himself easily. Just when we think we hear his voice, we suddenly realize that what comes to our ears is only its echo from another room. The poet is usually absent from his poems; in his place there is an image, easily changeable and ultimately intangible. This is what happens in "Darius" as well: Cavafy sketches in the poem the portrait of a colleague of his, the poet Phernazis, in a staged historical moment. This fictional poet has his own manners in the poem and his own

character. However, what is the relation between the fictitious poet and the other poet, the creator to whom he owes his existence? The question remains in suspense in the poem. Or rather, before we have time to ask, Cavafy throws the question back: what is the relation between Phernazis and us? Thus, Phernazis, silent in reality, serves in the poem as a mirror: whoever looks into it sees, before everything else, his own face—whether he be a poet or a simple reader. There is then no other solution for us but to study the features of this face, which is equidistant from Cavafy and from us.

4. Before looking at Phernazis' face, we must heed the conditions established in the poem for the operation of our perception. The poem has many levels of perspective. At the very rear of the stage stands Darius, hypothetical ancestor of Mithridates. In front of him moves the poet Phernazis, along with his contemporary persons and events (Mithridates, the silenced messenger, the scarcely visible but threatening legionnaires of Rome). A third level in the poem is determined by the narrator Cavafy, holding in his hands the date of the composition: 1920. Finally, in front of all that perfect staging stands the listener to the poem, part participant in its action, a changing person, each time with a different chronological identity. How does Phernazis' face appear through all these refractions?

When the poem begins Phernazis is busy working on his epic. He is writing about Darius. It is his intention to exalt thus indirectly the country's king, Mithridates, already laden with many glories; another glory to be added now, by emphasizing his descent from the great Darius. Is, then, Phernazis a mere sycophant, a flatterer of the powerful? Let us not hasten to draw such an easy conclusion; if so, a similar judgment should also fall on Pindar himself and on many other significant and famous poets of ancient, or even of more recent, times. Let us say, rather, that Phernazis is a professional poet, not a "disinterested" artist who follows only his Muse's commands. After all, the man is writing an epic—it is well known that epics, since Homeric times, are to be heard in royal courts.

That Phernazis is not a cheap sycophant is also shown by the very difficulty which stops him: he is asking himself about Darius' feelings, at the moment the Persian monarch seizes power. To determine the ultimate limits of Darius' psychology, Phernazis lets his hero waver

between arrogance (and intoxication) and realization of the vanity
of grandeur. Granted the latter limit is in praise of Mithridates, would
the former (arrogance and intoxication—a form of *hubris* in ancient
Greece) have flattered the king of Pontus? Phernazis is philosophizing,
not speech-making.

Suddenly, however, momentous news arrives: war. Cavafy's careful
formulation on this point ("the war with the Romans has begun")
shows that the storm does not break entirely unexpectedly. There already had been warning clouds in the sky. But Phernazis is dumbfounded; he did not expect this misfortune now. He thought time was
on his side. Thus, initially the catastrophe stimulates only his reflexes
as a poet: How can Mithridates now find the inclination to pay attention to Phernazis' epic, especially one written in Greek ("in the middle
of a war—just think, Greek poems!")? The ironic tone, not altogether
missing at the start of the poem (Phernazis' philosophical profundity
and his deep meditation sounded even there somewhat equivocally),
is now heard more clearly. Nevertheless, irony is not derived so much
from Phernazis' gestures as from the situation itself. It is the framework of war that makes Phernazis' moves ridiculous. In the last analysis, the problem is how to adapt to an unexpected and unpleasant
reality. Who can do it easily and immediately? Phernazis' reflexes
therefore function naturally and automatically. Personal concern initially overshadows collective misfortune. Such a spectacle is strange,
annoying, or even comical, when we are in a position to watch it
in others. Our tone, however, and our disposition automatically change
the moment we bring Phernazis' mask closer to our own face. We
discover with surprise how well it fits.

The poet Phernazis does not go easily beyond his personal concerns.
In this critical moment he remembers his own circle: his envious critics.
He had believed that with this epic he would have won the battle;
he would have risen high, overwhelming his colleagues. The war
thwarts or, rather, postpones (another surprising detail which shows
the depths of Cavafy's psychological insight into his poetic personages)
this well-planned project.

Phernazis' ambition here risks appearing like professional pretention.
However, before condemning Phernazis we must search Cavafy's
poetry to see how his colleagues behave in less critical moments: Dam-

mon, for instance, in "Dionysus' Escort," the Sculptor from Tyaneia, the engraver in the "Philhellene," or the unknown man from Edessa in "He Himself." What is needed specifically is not an ideal measure—which poet, dead or alive, would embody it in full?—but a realistic one. Thus measured, Phernazis is not so pretentious or so naive. Let us remember, moreover, that in these verses and those that follow Phernazis is not speaking directly—otherwise he would have known how to express himself more elegantly. His thoughts and words are snatched by a prompter who transmits them to us without any pretense. But the prompter's forthright gesture exposes Phernazis, who now grimaces perplexedly or even amusingly—for us the innocent, as Cavafy would say.

Phernazis finally does come out of his poetic cage; he begins to react like a common citizen of Amisus. The instinct of self-preservation now begins to function. It is expressed in a collective language: Phernazis plays the role of the citizen with a phraseology not lacking in affectation. Expressions such as "very well fortified" and "the Romans are the most awful enemies" betray a pedantry frayed into political rhetoric. It is not Phernazis' fault. As a poet he knew how to speak better. It is the fault of that damn war and the Roman legionnaires.

But Phernazis does not fully lose his poetic inspiration in the war's confusion. His mind works on a double level: with the common man's reflexes, on the one hand; with the poet's reflexes, on the other. What is strange is that the former now assist the latter, and the hard labor of the beginning now ends in birth: "arrogance and intoxication is what Darius must have felt." Darius? Or is it Phernazis, and others like him, and like us?

At the very start the poem presupposes quiet waters. The first whirlpool appears with Phernazis' dilemma concerning Darius' feelings; the second, much more intense and much wider, with the announcement of the war. However, while this second circle besieges the first, it does not immediately cancel it. It encircles it tightly until from its center arrogance and intoxication leap up, to soak not only Darius but Phernazis as well, and us, too.

What other cause could have resolved Phernazis' dilemma in favor of arrogance and intoxication, if not the warlike atmosphere which has intervened? Thus, arrogance passes from Darius to Mithridates, throws its shadow on the Roman legionnaires, and in the end covers Phernazis himself. His inability to participate more actively in the historical event, caused by the self-centered psychology of man in general and the poet in particular, finds its poetic name in the conclusion of the poem with "arrogance and intoxication." At this point indeed the word "intoxication" acquires a more concrete meaning when applied to the poet Phernazis, a meaning which it did not have in the beginning of the poem when it related to Darius' psychology.

Phernazis does not finish his poem on Darius. His deposition, however, concerning his tragicomic case helps Cavafy finish his own poem. Poets know that it is men who are deceived, not poems. To be completed, a poem requires total sincerity from its poet; otherwise it does not come out right, or if it does, it grimaces in protest against its imperfections. To tell his truth, a truth which of course depends on events and is not absolute, Cavafy needed Phernazis' mask. Cavafy himself may be hiding behind this mask, or perhaps we, readers of the poem, are. Phernazis, for his part, is totally sincere and realistic. Or is it that in the last analysis the same person is involved, since Phernazis is an imaginary personage? I do not wish to assert, of course, that Cavafy should be identified with Phernazis. Yet they are both poets and they share a common characteristic: they cannot create poetry without telling the truth, however bitter. This is their arrogance, the most innocuous form of arrogance that I know.

I fear the reader may be left somewhat puzzled and unsatisfied. He read an essay on "The Poet and History" expecting to find a portrait of a poet more robust than that of Phernazis. After all, the latter's participation in historical action is proved to be very limited, if not negative. I regret being the cause of the reader's disappointment. But I believe that in every effort our first step is self-knowledge. Everything else follows.

translated by A. A. Fatouros;
for S.N. and P.A.Z.

Athos NIKOS KASDAGLIS

13 June 1967

Parnassus, sky-blue in the distance. Solid and beautiful.

At Kaména Voúrla you think of Thermopylae. The mountain falls sheer, very close to the sea.

Thermopylae disappoints. Silt and debris have formed a low plain totally incompatible with one's vision of the terrible pass. Two tourist women admire a statue of Leonidas that reminds me of nothing.

The men who chose death over compromise would have wondered at such an evaluation.

We pass through the Vale of Tempe at night.

14 June 1967

In Salonica we see Aheropíitos, a strangely bare basilica with excessively ornate columns. They startle my eye, accustomed to Hellenic simplicity.

Saint Sophia is just the opposite. Huge and ornate—the decorated columns fit here. You feel insignificant beneath the huge dome with the marvelously preserved mosaics. There is a Virgin against a gold background above the main gate to the Sanctuary.

There are few frescoes, surprising in a church like this. We have no time to see anything else.

Nikos Kasdaglis

The trip to Ouranoúpolis, over the mountains, is beautiful. A hundred and ten kilometers of paved road, twenty-six of dirt. Athos appears in the distance above a peaceful headland with low contours.

Ierissós is a miserable village, choking in the dust of the plain. Ouranoúpolis has green, and lovely houses, as well as some hotels.

The captain of the *Saint Nikólaos,* on which we'll sail to Daphne, the arsanás* of Karyai, is in a hurry. He shouts that he'll leave us behind, but in the end waits.

There are shoals in the sea around Ouranoúpolis. As we pass into the waters of Athos it deepens abruptly.

The first monastery we come to is Thivaidha—called Kamena. It is deserted, but the church has been preserved.

Further along are skítes and cells,† then the monasteries of Dohiaríou and Xenofóndos. And the great monastery of Saint Panteleímon, the Russian monastery.

Its belfries are capped by typical Russian domes, which do not blend into the Greek landscape with its olive-covered mountains and golden harvest.

The size of the monasteries is impressive. One cell of the Russian monastery has six floors; it looks like a huge hotel. A section is preserved, but the rest is collapsing, roofless, with door and window frames missing. Next to it is another building with five floors; built of sturdy slate, they resist decay in spite of neglect.

Daphne, two hours from Ouranoúpolis, is disappointing. There's a jetty and a handful of dirty stores run by greedy owners, who would love to take your last cent.

Brief formalities regarding our entrance into Mount Athos follow. They return our identity cards with instructions to present ourselves to the police station at Karyai.

I had thought we would be going on foot, and had figured the distance to be six to seven kilometers on the map. Of course it was already

* The small harbor of the monastery. It consists of a small landing-stage and a small fortresslike warehouse, which could offer some resistance to the pirates that plagued the Aegean.

† Small cells are built for a single monk, who has renounced worldly things and the company of his fellow men; a cell can be not only a monk's room in a monastery, but the whole building that houses the monks.

obvious that we would be passing over a mountain, and I guessed what kind it would be.

Fortunately there is a bus. In fact the mountain is precipitous and wooded, a real jungle. The distance, with the curves, is fourteen kilometers. The road is bad and rises steeply; the bus labors.

On the way, near Daphne, is the monastery of Ksiropótamos. As we climb the ridge we see Karyai and the monastery of Koutloumousíou below us, multicolored like something out of a fairy tale. Way behind us, towering precipitously, wild, Mount Athos.

It's almost an hour before we get to Karyai.

New formalities to get a residence permit which assures us of one or two days' hospitality at each monastery. The monasteries are twenty, not counting the skites.

We ask for Professor Milonas. They point to Protátos, the church of the senior abbot.*

It's a basilica of average size, with wall paintings up to the level of the highest windows. Above that are plaster and wooden beams. Vespers are going on as we enter, and we can only steal glances at the closest of the paintings.

I know so little about painting that I do not suspect I am among the marvels of Byzantine iconography. When vespers are over I shall see the Protátos through the eyes of Mr. Milonas, who is perched up on a scaffold, beneath the ceiling. He is taking photographs.

After the liturgy, he shows us the frescoes of the Protátos, done by Pansélinos in the fourteenth century, and asks us to compare the quality of the work. In short, I learn to see Byzantine painting.

We discuss the possibility of leaving for the monastery of Ivíron. They look at us quizzically, and explain that the monasteries close their doors at the twelfth hour, Mount Athos time. The twelfth is not a fixed hour—it coincides with sunset. One monastery—I forget which—measures time from sunrise.

When the monasteries close their doors, we will have neither food nor shelter. We cannot leave, and a modern iconographer takes us in; he has a pretty house. The wooden balcony has a view toward

* Mount Athos is governed by the abbots of the twenty monasteries. The prokathímenos, the senior abbot, is elected for one year.

Athos, and my eyes show such longing that we are asked if we intend
to climb it. We have no time; our days are numbered.

"Don't worry," they insist. "Come back on July 4. There's a fair
at the chapel on the summit."

"The fourth of July is pretty close," we smile back.

"Not so; on Athos we follow the old calendar."

Proud of his art, both monastic and lay, the icon painter shows
us his work. He says he wants to shake off the influence of tradition,
but unfortunately he has too many orders for a particular composition:
a head of Christ painted to appear old. The icon painter does not
sell it as antique, but it's easy to foresee that the deception takes place
at second hand.

15 June 1967

I wake at six in the morning, my usual hour. By the time the others
are up and ready and we are all treated to coffee, it's eight-thirty.

We pause at a shop with souvenirs of Athos, a tourist business like
all the others, neither better nor worse. Two pieces of ornate wood
carving are on display only, not for sale. Anyway, they are examples
of Eastern art, with nothing to do with Athos. A monk is the salesman,
and pretty sharp too.

We set off for the monastery of Ivíron. We were to leave at dawn.
Normally it's an hour and a quarter away; we say two, in spite of
it being downhill.

We are disappointed at the monastery. We are greeted with indifference, aside from the arhontáris,* who treats us to the traditional raki
with a sweet and coffee, then forgets all about us. They have just
finished showing a group of officers around, and nobody is in the mood
to bother with us.

We show exaggerated interest in the food. There's plenty, and it's
good, in spite of my brother's grumbling that he doesn't eat fish.

After the meal we try to have a look round the monastery, but
everything is locked. The monks are asleep or about to go to sleep.
Only the arhontáris pays any attention to us. He is an Athenian bum
who ended up a monk, though he had no faith at all. He'd sworn to his

* The monk responsible for looking after monastery's guests.

father never to do a stroke of work, planning to become a priest somewhere abroad. He failed at the Theological schools of Rizários and
Athonáidha, which was no surprise. He found the answer by
becoming a monk. Now, in his conversation, he mixes broken English
and French.

He shows us to a miserable cell with filthy beds and bedclothes,
and asks us to excuse the untidiness. It's *le dernier*, he says in French.
His use of the language rings unpleasantly.

He cannot help us see the monastery. The monks are suspicious
to a degree, and their suspicion appears unshakable. Theft is an everyday event on Athos.

Finally we find the sexton. He opens the church and we see it
hurriedly in the dark. Not much to see anyway; he's anxious to get
rid of us.

The monastery has a famous library. We won't see it; the caique
for the monastery of the Greatest Lavra departs at four-thirty. If we
stay we'll see Ivíron properly, because there's another crowd of army
officers coming. The monks predict that the caique for Lavra won't
come because it's stormy.

I can't see any sign of a storm, and we have no wish to stay. The
caique arrives right on time; it connects with the bus from Karyai.

Ivíron is idiorhythmic,* and the monks certainly show their independence. We agree, it should have been called a *rebet asker*.†

As we sail around Athos, we see in the distance the monastery of
Karakálos, the boundary of Lavra territory. It's wooded right down
to the base of the mountain; the sea is serene and crystal clear. The
small port of Morfonós, where they are loading timber, belongs to
Lavra too.

We see the great monastery from afar, built 150 meters up the
mountain. Attached to the arsanás is a concrete tower, which doesn't
match, an eyesore. They explain that it's just a layer of concrete added
to preserve the old tower; the damage has been done.

They tell us to wait at the arsanás and a truck will come to pick

* In such a monastery the monk is free to worship when he will, has a private life
and a personal income, eats and cooks apart from the others, and so on. He can even
have a servant—another monk—if his financial state permits.
† Literally, Turkish irregular troops; metaphorically it means "chaos."

us up. The monastery is half an hour away. We shrug and walk on in the company of a Greek-American. We thought Mount Athos meant walking. Today only the eccentric walk.

At Lavra we are greeted with the same indifference. We inquire about the truck; we had not met it along the way. Oh, they say, the driver must be somewhere around. He'll take it and drive down to the arsanás.

That's our first impression. The porter who checks our permits leads us to the reception room. The arhontáris is a salaried layman, who does his job professionally, conscientiously. The rooms and beds are clean, as is the refectory. The food is ascetic, nourishing without giving any pleasure. Maybe there's an ulterior motive. Perhaps the monastery pays the arhontáris a fixed sum for each guest, so the less a guest costs, the more he pockets. We have settled and are roaming round the monastery when the pilgrims who stayed down at the arsanás begin to trickle in. They waited furiously for the truck, got fed up, and have angrily arrived on foot.

Someone whispers that we're in luck: some monks have come from Ivíron and will be shown the treasure. This is a rare and priceless privilege. While the keys to the treasure are being fetched, we're shown the library. Two and a half thousand hand-written and illuminated manuscripts. The most valuable are behind glass, open at some choice page, samples of a marvelous art. It does not occur to us to leaf through the pages of even the lesser manuscripts. Lovingly buried on the shelves, they seldom show their leatherbound backs.

The treasure has three huge locks, and the keys are kept by three of the proistámeni. It can be opened only in the presence of the three key-bearers.

The room is crammed with carefully folded, gold-embroidered vestments. In two of the showcases are spread out a cassock, a miter, and one or two pieces more, the only things we can see.

The showcases round the walls are packed with treasures. Here and there we make out a priceless chalice or censer. We pass into the rooms beyond, but it has already grown dark.

Displayed behind glass are bibles with precious stones and mosaic covers . . . bishop's staffs and archbishops' clasps studded with pearls.

Chrysobulls of Byzantine Emperors and carved wooden crosses embossed with gold. We suspect a mythical treasure lies in the darkness. Someone has a flashlight, and we crowd round.

Hastily, having assured themselves we are Orthodox, they take us to pay our respects to the sacred relics and the tomb of St. Athanasius, founder of the monastery. In the dark we can see nothing of the large, famous church, and the relics do not interest me.

Outside the church they show us the tombs of three Patriarchs of Constantinople: narrow cells with a few icons and a holy light.

In the chapel of St. Athanasius they show us the huge, heavy cross he wore. This was his personal cell, later converted into a chapel. Novices are welcomed into the monastery in this chapel.

One by one the pilgrims hang the massive cross round their necks and pick up the two iron pastoral staffs, while the priest murmurs a prayer. Some of the visitors delicately refuse to take part in a ceremony meaningless to them, and the monks perceive this.

The eternal problem of understanding—that precious gift you offer willingly—you see the others refusing to give, or accepting with condescension.

The atmosphere cools; the arhontáris informs us that the caique for Ierissós will sail very early next morning, at six. I explain that our group—there are three of us—plan to go the other way, to go round Athos. He shakes his head. A caique won't go around until three days from now, he says, and the monastery can offer hospitality for only twenty-four hours.

I feel like an intruder, particularly after the cold reception we got at Ivíron. I reply drily that we'll leave on foot before the twenty-four hours are up, and, in any case, we'd like to see the monastery.

He softens immediately. He did not mean to say that the monastery would throw us out if we needed to stay. We could stay two or even more days.

Meanwhile my brother returns. He has met a monk he knew, a man who edited his book on Athos.

The símandron* for matins wakes me at two in the morning. I woke at the first sharp blow on the iron símandron. Then I

---

* Wooden or metal blocks hammered against each other; they antedate bells.

hear the call of the small, wooden símandron. Rhythmical to start with, then fast, very fast, furious. The summons is heard three times.

I will come to love the sound of the símandron during the few days of my stay.

16 June 1967

I am alone in the reception room when a venerable old monk, gentle and soft-spoken, comes up. I recognize him. I had known of his disability. It's Father Alexandros, whom my brother had gone to see. I rise and he introduces himself.

He's an important person on Athos: chief secretary to the Epistasía, the governing body of Athos, until his disability forced him to withdraw. Today he is one of the twelve elders of Lavra.

Lavra, an idiorhythmic monastery, is ruled by twelve elders, who hold the post for life. When one dies, his replacement is elected by those remaining eleven—a real oligarchy. The same men also elect the three members of the executive body, who run the day-to-day matters of the monastery.

As he's disabled, I offer to look for my brother, who is wandering about the monastery somewhere, but he won't let me. Let's have a coffee first, then we can look for him together.

The old man's presence immediately changes the mood. Most of the guests have already left, at six in the morning, only the three of us and the Greek-American stayed. The arhontáris becomes affable, almost friendly. He does not mention the length of our stay at the monastery.

By the time we have finished our coffee, my brother and our friend return. More monks gather round. As we talk we learn that the monastery's generator has broken down, and they have no electricity. Our friend, an electrical engineer, offers to repair it, and they accept gratefully. An electrical engineer in these deserted parts is a stroke of unbelievable luck—Divine Providence almost. Could he perhaps also fix their water-driven generator so that they can do without the diesel-powered one? They go off to measure the water in the dammed stream, and I try to make myself useful by giving agricultural tips.

They no longer are entertaining us out of obligation. We are friends
of the monastery. The monks, isolated from the world, have an incredible need to open their hearts. When our engineer returns, we
are led to the great reception hall, used only for dignitaries, and they
ask us to sign the visitor's book. There, on the first page is the signature
of King Paul.

From the window they point out the seat of Emperor Nicephorus
Phocas, who had asked them to prepare this beautiful cell so he could
find peace after his troubled years of ruling the Empire. He never
made it; the news reached the monastery that the Emperor had died.

We make a great show of admiring this room, with its carved arm-
chairs, recently brought over from Crete, embroidered cloths on the
tables, and the paintings on the walls. Tidy as a well-kept home. There
are also wood-carvings made on holy Athos and contemporary carvings
from Jerusalem. Each must have taken years of work, but the result
is mediocre. On the wall a framed diploma looks as if it were printed,
even to our eyes, accustomed to proofreading. But when we examine
it close up, we realize it has been done by hand, the work of an incredible calligrapher, who must have taken God-knows-what pains over
it.

This reception hall is dear to the monastery, and it would be rude
to show how little interested we are. Doors on either side of a corridor.
It must be the guesthouse for the VIPs.

They soon repay us. They inform us we'll visit the Katholikón,
the great church of Lavra, painted by the iconographer Theophanes
the Cretan in the sixteenth century. We had seen it the day before,
but in the dark. Architecturally it is an elaborate church, with entrance
and chapel. The sexton and an ordained monk, the deacon Ezekiel,
accompany us, and this is unusual. We quickly realize what an excep-
tional favor it is. I don't know what education the deacon has had,
but his mind is keen and brilliant. He burns with passion for Byzantine
iconography, and knows it well. He loves this church, and is profoundly
attached to it.

"The tradition of the monastery," he tells us, "claims that it was
Theophanes who painted the entire church, and when he died his
son continued the work. Look at that part over there: surely it's by

Theophanes' hand. But the saint next to it—how could the same man have painted that? It tells me nothing. And the one beyond that? The monastery's tradition holds that Theophanes did the whole church; what can I say?"

He shows us the iconostasis; it's marble, the gift of a Czar in 1887. It has flaking, badly painted icons. In order to set it up, they had to tear down the old sixteenth-century wood-carved iconostasis with its marvelous paintings. They hacked it to bits, and whatever paintings were salvaged were hung on the walls of the church as icons. Below the marble iconostasis, two beautiful twelfth-century icons (a gift of the Emperor Andronicus, if I remember correctly) make the contrast even sharper.

We admire the Pantocrator on the central dome, and the other paintings. The Last Supper, recently cleaned, is on the left pediment. Ezekiel looks at it pensively; he does not approve of cleaning icons. Outside, in the entry hall, are more recent paintings. Ezekiel shrugs without further comment.

A beautifully painted marble holy water font stands in the courtyard.

"A skilled copyist," the deacon tells us. "Whoever sees it thinks it was done in the sixteenth century, but I know it was done in the eighteenth. The faces are Byzantine, but the line is different."

From there they take us to the monastery's second church, the Panaghiá Koukouzélissa. After emerging from the overly ornate Katholikón it seems humble, naively painted by a lay iconographer in the eighteenth century. Ezekiel does not accompany us.

Tradition holds that Panaghiá Koukouzélissa miraculously puts out fires,* and the sexton asserts it faithfully.

They call us for the midday meal. After that the monks sleep, and at two in the morning they wake up for matins. I take my brother for a walk outside the fortress of the monastery. Disappointment. The area round the massive walls is a rubbish dump. The huge orchard with the morello cherry, walnut, and almond trees, is abandoned. Water flows in neglected irrigation ditches.

We attend their devout vespers from four to five-thirty. A venerable

* Fire always has been, and still is, the scourge of Mount Athos.

eighty-five-year-old monk, a former surgeon, is chanting. There is
nothing theatrical in the ceremony; everybody takes part.

After vespers, we go from cell to cell. They want to treat us. There
are two compatriots of ours from the Dodecanese: the monk Efraim,
polite, good-hearted, from Maritsán—came as a pilgrim and stayed—is
humble and mild. And the monk Abbakoum from the island of Sími.
Passionate and undisciplined, he had time enough to live an Odyssey
before he was twenty-five. He tried to enter other monasteries, but
never managed it. Hot-tempered and abrupt, he succeeded in getting
himself expelled from Athos twice, but always made his way back.
He has been a monk for forty-eight years, now is a trapesáris, keeper
of the monastery's foodstores.

Monk Efraim enters the refectory humbly. Old Alexandros, he says,
is outside looking for us.

"Tell him to wait," Abbakoum snaps. "I have guests."

To smooth things over my brother makes an excuse and leaves,
while I remain with Abbakoum. His favor is indispensable if we want
to see the refectory. It's too late now, and we plan to see it tomorrow
in the morning light.

After dinner Ezekiel meets us in the reception room. If our friend
succeeds in repairing the generator, he'll have the nerve to ask the
epítropi (members of the executive body) to show us the room which
houses the icons. They don't open it to just anyone, because the icons
have been neither arranged nor classified, but if the generator is put
right, they'll be under obligation to us. He reckons there are more
than six hundred Byzantine icons there, dating from the ninth century
to the Fall of Constantinople. The monastery's generator now becomes
an object of unexpected interest.

We tell him that tomorrow night we will sleep in the monastery
of Saint Dionísios, and ask what we should request to see there. Ezekiel
makes ironic comments about the other monastery and its comforts.
The Abbot has a motorboat, can hit thirty miles an hour, and does
in fact take pleasure trips in it.

"Thirty miles an hour? But it must be a Criss-Craft! Where did
he get it?"

Ezekiel smiles condescendingly. Dionísios is a kinóvion monastery,
you know, and the abbot is absolute master in these places.

17 June 1967

My friend disappears in the morning to see to the generator, and the venerable Alexandros comes to the reception room to keep us company. He shows us his flowers, which he loves passionately. He grows them and sends them to other monasteries too. Then he shows us his stamps, and I try to work up some interest; my brother manages much better. I calculate we've lost more than two hours, and we're leaving at noon. Will we have time to see the refectory and the paintings?

Finally our engineer arrives. He has failed with the generator; the damage cannot be patched up so easily. Monkish deals are clear and simple: we will not see the icons. We're left with the refectory, thanks to the favor we've gained with Abbakoum.

First he treats us, then shows us into the enormous hall with the marble tables—we reckon that two hundred and fifty people can eat comfortably here. Abbakoum's favor has its surprises. He delivers a long sermon for our benefit, taking his cue from the icons. He knows the Four Gospels, the Holy Scriptures, the hymns, the Apocalypse, and I don't know what else, by heart. He talks rapidly, reciting the holy texts and commenting on them in his Simian accent, and gets furious if he imagines we aren't paying enough attention; every now and then he calls us to order.

We worry lest we miss seeing the frescoes. He might lead us out after he's finished his sermon, so we steal surreptitious looks at whatever we can.

We're wrong. He finishes and leaves us alone to see the scenes from the Apocalypse and the icons, commenting that we would be better off to pay attention to his words, because in the future we can see the paintings as much as we like, but we'll never have another chance to hear his sermon. Later, we learn that the sermon, too, was an unusual favor. Whenever new pilgrims arrive, he just shows them into the refectory and bustles off, without giving them any more attention.

We miss Ezekiel.

We say goodbye to the friends we've made in the monastery and go to the reception room for the midday meal. Afterward we will leave for Lavra, and all the monks will go to sleep, tired after matins.

Father Alexandros' assistant searches us out to ask a favor. His brother is seriously ill in a hospital in Piraeus. He wants us to take the best doctor to examine him. We try to explain how a big hospital functions. He is disappointed, thinks we do not want to help him.

In the arsanás of Lavra we begin to worry that the caique won't come. They told us two, it's a quarter past already, and we know that caiques are always on time. We find the guard, who lives in the station at the arsanás. The caique will arrive at a quarter to three, he says; the monks don't understand the meaning of time. Just look at the way they measure it!

The caique arrives at a quarter of three sharp. We're the only passengers; an unscheduled boat had passed through two hours before.

We circumnavigate Athos. A precipitous and massive mountain, it pours its cliffs down to the sea, which deepens abruptly. We pick up a monk along the way. He points out his cell, which is completely isolated halfway up a towering cliff-face.

"How does he get up there?" There's a footpath. He has to climb the ridge of course. He doesn't get food from the monastery, so what does he offer the monastery to feed him? The cell has its own hazel nut and olive trees, and a few almond. It has beehives too, so he gets by. As for water, he collects rain water in a cistern.

"How are cells distributed?" There's a monkish system. The cell is given to the monk free, but he, however, makes a bequest to the monastery—whatever he can. As long as he lives, the monastery gives him the income from the bequest in food on the basis of six percent. When he dies the bequest reverts to the monastery. Aside from that, it's whatever he can make for himself, from the earnings of the cell.

Kapsokalívia is built on a precipitous and verdant mountainside. Trees are planted in terraces, and there must be water. Below Kapsokalívia the rocks take strange shapes, like sculptured stalactites. The arsanás is in a nearby harbor, so that the steps can descend gently. Further along there's the island of Christóforos—a barren rock with a chapel.

We arrive at the skíti of Saint Anna—at its arsanás, that is, because the skíti is perched on the mountain, an hour's walk away. The caique stops here; it will leave in the morning in two days. On the slope above the arsanás stand cells and one or two chapels.

We've been advised not to stay at the skíti of Saint Anna, which has nothing of special interest, but to go to the monastery of Dionísios.

After brief haggling with the captain, he takes us to Dionísios for eighty drachmas. He will return to Saint Anna because he has his normal run at six-thirty in the morning. On the way we pass the monastery of Saint Pávlos and from afar we see the monastery of Símonos Pétra, high up on the mountain, a true eyrie. No cells or trees surround it, as they do at other monasteries. There is only an inhospitable precipice all around.

A headland hides Símonos Pétra from us as we sail into the arsanás of Dionísios. Here, too, the monastery is built on a precipice ten minutes from the arsanás, but the landscape is gentler.

Wanting to gossip a bit, we ask a monk at the arsanás where their motorboat is. He looks at us in surprise.

"The motorboat? What motorboat? You must mean the one the monastery once had. It's been almost thirty years since we sold it. However did you remember it?"

The ravine that leads to the monastery is thick with walnut trees. At the bottom of the ravine, the monastery's livestock: horses and mules graze free, bells hanging from their necks. The stable is next to the arsanás.

The cobbled path is expertly built and well-maintained, with a fountain and benches here and there, as in a park. After what we'd heard at Lavra, we wonder at the spirit of cleanliness.

Vespers and sounding as we enter the monastery reception room. The reception room is spotless—it's not just the neatness that impresses us, the monastery is rich. They offer us preserves, coffee and raki and lead us to a cell. The beds have spring mattresses and attractive spreads. We drop our belongings and hasten to vespers.

Outside the refectory, a covered passageway, open to the landscape on one side, has fine icons. We pause at the refectory door. It is made of heavy, black wood, ornately carved, and still survives, in spite of the woodworm. In other monasteries the frames of the doors and windows are often changed in a slipshod fashion.

Vespers is devout. The door of the church is also heavy and carved, and the interior is very dark. The light seeping in is dim, since the monastery is built in the shadow of the mountain, down in the ravine. We console ourselves with the thought that it might be brighter in the morning, and there'll be time enough, before the caique arrives at seven.

We return to the reception room to admire the panorama of the verdant ravine and the setting sun. Its reflection along the coast line is blinding. The ravine, full of nightingales.

Later, at supper time, we go to see the paintings outside the refectory. This is a kinóvion monastery and the monks eat together. They invite us to follow the "lesson"—which is what they call their meal.

We sit at one side. The scene is impressive. The refectory is barely lit, the monks are seated at two long marble tables, with a lectern between them for the reader. He reads a text from the Holy Scriptures in a deep, severe voice; it is beautiful. When he comes to the end, we hear an order that sounds almost like a military command. The monks rise, stand in rows, and leave the refectory. An army mess hall is run with much milder regulations.

The Abbot notices us and invites us to his quarters for a glass of water. "What do you think of our monastery?" he asks amicably, revealing his secret pride.

He is an aristocrat, with a pleasant face. We say we like it a lot.

"It's nice. A bit cramped; built on the precipice."

His living quarters are perhaps the best room in the monastery. It has windows on three sides, which overlook the sea and ravine. Half of the space consists of an enclosed balcony. The Abbot orders our water to be brought in.

The atmosphere is entirely different from Lavra. There the elders had to beg in order to get something done. Here the Abbot is absolute master. The treat arrives: Turkish delight, raki, and coffee, as elsewhere. But the glasses are clean, the raki good, and the coffee delicious.

The Abbot chatters on pleasantly. He speaks about his trips outside. Athos, and his conversation sparkles with caustic comments. He knows what is going on in lay Greece, and this impresses us—most of Athos' inhabitants might as well be from the moon.

He asks if we would like to smoke; smoking, he says, is allowed in his quarters. A subtle way of insinuating that it is forbidden everywhere else in the monastery. A monk enters; some merchant is waiting to see the Abbot.

"Tell him to wait. I'll see him later."

He discovers we have just come from Lavra, and grows pensive.

"A fine monastery, yes, very fine. Except, well, they're idiorhythmic. Here in the kinóvion we all eat in the common refectory, the same food, from the Abbot to the last novice. Take cassocks, for instance: I order forty, different sizes, but they're identical in material and make. Each chooses the one that fits him best. Our socks are the same, so are our shoes and everything else. In Lavra the monk gets three kilos of olive oil a year, and the elders get ten. How can such things be justified? Aren't we all monks? Over there, each has his own table."

The rivalry between Lavra and Dionísios is obvious, but this man is more persuasive because he's more intelligent.

The arhontáris enters and announces that the guests' supper is ready.

"Fine," the Abbot interrupts, "they'll be coming shortly."

He keeps us a little longer. They have an all-night liturgy after supper and it will be beautiful. Why don't we drop in for an hour or so?

He allows us to take our leave. His authority over the monastery is benign, but heavy. Strict paternalism.

We're late; the other guests are already eating in the reception area. The food is frugal, but well-prepared, home-cooked. There's even salad, an unheard-of luxury on Athos. The arhontáris is attentive, alert lest we need something. Two monks, guests of the monastery, are eating with us. One has attached himself to a group of theology students. His manner of speech is obviously effeminate.

We ask the arhontáris what time the vigil starts. He looks bewildered. On Athos time is counted differently from the outside world. The liturgy starts at the first night hour, Athos time, and ends at the eighth.

We work that out as being almost quarter to nine. Only my brother will go. Our friend and I prefer to get some sleep; apart from the trip by caique, we'll have eleven hours of driving to do after noon.

18 June 1967

We wake in the morning and dash off to the church. The monks are asleep, exhausted from their vigils. We admire the paintings outside

the refectory until the time of our departure. A priest comes to open
the church and sees us. He goes in to fetch miracle-working oil from
the saint's holy lamp. Have we paid our respects to the sacred relics?
No we have not; we arrived late last night.

He ushers us to the right-hand side of the sancturay. There we
wait for him to bring the relics. We kiss them, then ask his permission
to see the church. He nods with some displeasure; he had not expected
us to bother him at that hour of the morning.

We are disappointed: the church is too dark at that hour. The sun
must rise pretty high before its light reaches the monastery in the
ravine. We can hardly see a thing. High on the iconostasis we can
just about pick out an icon. We ask if it is old. The light has fooled
us; it's a photograph of an old icon.

We are wasting time in the gloom, and we leave so as not to detain
the priest unnecessarily. At the monastery of Dionísios, one of the
finest, we saw only the paintings outside the refectory.

The caique is down at the arsanás at exactly seven o'clock. It's
packed; everyone's going to Daphne. As we sail past, we all admire
Símonos Pétra once again.

At Daphne we ask when the caique for Ouranoúpolis leaves. Between
ten-thirty and eleven, we're told. So we have time to see the nearby
monastery of Ksiropótamos. Nevertheless, we take the precaution of
asking the guard who checks our identity cards.

"The caique leaves at exactly nine-thirty."

"But the monks told us ten-thirty to eleven."

"Don't ask the monks. The caique leaves at exactly nine-thirty."

We wait to find out who is right. The caique leaves at nine-thirty
sharp. We bid Athos farewell as we circumnavigate it. In two hours
we'll be at Ouranoúpolis, and after that we'll have to drive furiously
to get to Athens the same day.

On our way back we pass through the Vale of Tempe early in the
afternoon. Still dazzled by Athos, I give it an indifferent glance.

translated by N. C. Germanakos

The Plaster Cast   THANASIS VALTINOS

They laid me on a wheeled stretcher. They stripped me, cutting
off my trousers and underwear with scissors to keep from hurting
me. The nurse said they were going to take X-rays. She was still
young, and cheerful. I asked if this would mean another ordeal.

"No," she said. "They won't even move you."

She walked ahead, opening the doors wide so we could pass.

The laboratory was dim and smelled of mildew and chemicals. It
took several seconds before my eyes got used to the light. I could
make out the doctor, shielded by his lead apron, readying the equipment. He was stooped over, working in silence. Before long he signaled
the nurse to move out of the way and a metal arm began to move
back and forth along the length of my body. I sensed that there were
more people in the room. I thought I heard whispering behind me
and turned my head to see. Just then, as though they had been waiting
for this moment, someone shouted: "Take." It wasn't the doctor. I
heard a lever being lowered and immediately—if I can say that—felt
the rays bore through my flesh and bones.

This happened four or five times. They X-rayed my knees, my pelvis,
my chest, my skull. Each time the metal arm moved into place with
surprising accuracy and speed. The whole procedure lasted less than
three minutes. In the end it was the doctor who said: "okay"; we

were through. His voice sounded cold and impersonal, like a command. It expressed neither satisfaction or any kind of emotion.

I sighed with relief. As the door opened a draft struck my face, and the nurse wheeled me back out into the corridor. She was pushing from behind now, and I couldn't see her. I was moving, feet first, and could see only the walls of the endless corridor, gleaming and bare, passing by.

We ended up in a poorly lighted, low-ceilinged chamber. There was only one window, high up in a narrow wall; it had bars and reinforced glass. From the location of the window and the quality of the light I guessed we were in a basement room. The nurse placed me in the middle of the room, folded her arms across her chest and stood facing me. I asked what was next.

"They're studying the X-rays now," she said. "I think the operation will start soon."

She was still pleasant, but I noticed an indefinable change in her mood. I was afraid this was because I was asking questions.

I stopped and tried to shift my position on the table's hard surface. I felt my spine stretched taut like a bow. I tried to shift and suddenly a fierce pain in my left thigh surged through me. I bit my lip to keep from crying out; the nurse reached over and held my wrists with one hand, resting her other on my forehead, in an effort to keep me still.

"Be still," she said kindly. "You must be quiet; there's nothing to be gained any other way."

I realized she was right and told her so. It was clear that in my condition any movement at all was not only useless but damaging as well.

She began to stroke my brow tenderly, almost maternally.

"You must be patient," she continued. "Patience. It's a difficult lesson, but in these times it's necessary for us all to learn it."

I let her stroke my forehead. It felt good. I needed comforting and she knew it. I'm also sure she knew she had quieted me. I was thirsty and asked for a glass of water.

"I'll bring it at once," she said, letting go of my wrists and forehead to leave. I could hear her heels along the corridor for a brief moment until they died away.

The Plaster Cast

I was alone. While waiting for her return, the events of the morning
leaped vividly to mind. The deafening compressor . . . the open drain-
age pipes . . . the pavement with the missing stone (that idiotic pavement) . . . later, slipping, and through the depths of my fainting,
the ambulance siren. It would have to happen to me! I choked back
the curse on my lips and, to calm the rage building inside me, deliberately forced myself to study the room.

Its walls were painted white—a repellent, plastic white. In the corner
to my right was a glass display case with surgical instruments and
directly above it an electric clock. I imagined the second hand silently
and precisely outlining its circle, but the glare reflecting from the
glass kept me from seeing the time. I raised my hand to look at my
own watch, then, for the first time, noted that it was broken and
had stopped. Though not superstitious, this seemed an ill omen, and
I was seized by an uncontrollable urge to know what time it was—as
though something important depended on it. I looked out the window
and tried to guess by the light. But the light no longer showed any
change whatsoever, as though it had frozen and was carved forever
in that corner, in that reinforced glass. Suddenly I felt a breath of
terror deep in my bowels. I remained motionless, hoping to catch some
sound from the outside. This was something new and had an immediate
effect: no sound reached this chamber from anywhere; waves of panic
broke over me. Before the cry of anguish could escape my lips, the
nurse returned. She indeed held a glass of water in her hand, but
I hadn't heard her coming and the suspicion lodged in my mind that
she had been waiting behind the door. She may have guessed this
from my expression, for I saw her eyelashes flutter with embarrass-
ment, though she quickly regained her composure. There must have
been beads of perspiration on my face because, without setting the
glass down, she pulled a tiny, perfumed handkerchief from her bosom
and wiped my face. Then she tried to help me drink, half lifting my
head carefully as if I were a baby. I refused to drink and told her
I was no longer thirsty. She showed no annoyance, set the glass down
in the corner next to the door, and resumed her stance across from
me. Only this time she said sadly: "you must trust me." And then
immediately, all professional: "The doctors are coming."

I heard their footsteps and the rustle of their jackets as they entered

155

the chamber. There were two of them, and they came and stood over me with their hands behind their backs, watching me for some time without speaking. They were the same height, a little above average, and probably the same age, but it was hard to tell because they were wearing caps and surgical masks. Of their faces only the eyes showed, nothing else.

I knew I had no open wound, and their attitude disturbed me. Forgetting I had just offended her—if my refusal to drink was offensive—I turned to the nurse, expecting at least a sign of encouragement. But she was bending over the case with the instruments and all I could see were her round buttocks and a bit of bare flesh between her deathly white stockings and the hem of her skirt. Then I stopped seeing anything.

Someone had pressed a button and the chamber was flooded with a harsh, stabbing light. I shielded my eyes with my hand and could see the two figures, and a third person in their midst, who immediately vanished.

It was strange that I hadn't been aware of my nakedness before, with the nurse. Now, in the blinding artificial light and under the scrutinizing eyes of the doctors, I felt exposed and defenseless. "Delivered into their hands," I thought, trying to make my head more comfortable on the surface of the table upon which I was prey. I turned sideways to avoid the blinding light, and through half-shut lids saw one of the two doctors, his head and chest bent back slightly, examining the X-rays which were still wet from developing. He held them briefly against the light, giving each a quick glance before passing them, one by one, to his partner. Then they left them somewhere, and the second doctor came over, grasped my chin, and turned my face toward him. It was the same gesture my father used when I was a boy, and instinctively I waited for the slap. Instead, with a swift experienced movement, he steadied his thumbs at the base of my nose and his fingers forcefully rolled back my eyelids and he examined their interiors. He released them immediately and through a swirling kaleidoscope I heard him say: "We can start." These were the first, and for a long time the only words that left their mouths.

When I finally succeeded in opening my eyes again, they had started working on my feet. The light bothered me less now, and I was able to raise my head from the nape of my neck somewhat and watch them. They worked quickly, silently, completely synchronized. The nurse, her back to me, held the soles of my feet rigid, at the height of her waist. Her stance struck me as a bit unnatural; she could easily have done the same job with a less strained appearance. It occurred to me that she was trying to avoid my glance and this disturbed me. But I took courage from the fact that, contrary to my expectations, until this moment I had suffered no pain. I watched the hands of the doctors moving with assurance and agility, and in spite of the mortification inflicted by their behavior, I had to admit that they knew their stuff.

They had wrapped my shins with plaster tapes—like World War I leggings—and were heading inexorably upward. The memory of the stabbing pain in my thigh made me cringe, figuring that the time was approaching when the tortures finally would begin. I held my breath and clenched my teeth in order to bear the wave of pain that was to come, but, strangely, nothing happened. I felt only the fingers of the doctor quickly feeling my muscles, then the pressure of the tape being applied and squeezing my skin, and, I confess, an odd tremor of excitement raced up my spine. The doctor must have noticed because he interrupted his work for a moment, threw me a quick glance, and whispered something which the other heard coldly, without expression.

The problems began when they reached my hips. Even for me, as yet unsuspecting, it was clear that if the bandaging were continued (if it was necessary to continue it), they would have to move me or at least to lift my body off the surface of the table in some way. With a morbid curiosity, and as though the matter did not concern me at all, I waited to see what would happen.

The doctors had stopped and had withdrawn to a corner for some kind of makeshift conference. I couldn't see them, I could only see the nurse who continued standing, rigid, holding the soles of my feet to her waist. I studied the line of her neck and her stooped shoulders, and suddenly I felt pity for her. My first impression, that she was

young and cheerful, was false. She was only a frightened, oppressed
creature, sentenced by some fate to a work she dreaded, which she
tried to cope with with whatever dignity remained in her. Regret began
to overcome me for my suspicions of her; I wanted to tell her so,
but was restrained by the thought that such a thing would be forbidden.
I tried to turn my head toward the doctors but couldn't see them.
I could sense them behind me, in the corner, communicating with
gestures and sign language. Not even a whisper could be heard, and
at this moment alarm struck like lightning: the two conspiring behind
me were planning my doom.

Before I could react they recognized my fear and I saw them descend
upon me. They grabbed my arms, still free, and a soft but unbelievably
strong and expertly trained hand clamped my mouth. I felt the
wedding band on the middle finger as my lip was forced unbearably
against my teeth, and in the throes of this sharp pain I heard the
dragging of a table and the thump of my feet as they placed them
on it. Then I saw the nurse approach with an enormous syringe in
her hand. She had the look of the Mater Dolorosa. It wasn't necessary
for her to strap down my arm. Already, from the way she held me
fast, my veins stood out like ropes. She leaned over me carefully, easily
found the right place, and struck me. I felt the strange liquid flowing
into me, at a different temperature from my own blood, and while
waiting for the syringe to empty I lost consciousness.

When I came to, they had plastered me all over. My stomach and
chest were a snow-white plateau and the outline of my pelvis was
swollen unnaturally. With my outrageous rump I imagined myself
looking a little like a roly-poly idol and a little like an astronaut in
a space suit. They had left only my face unsmeared, and probably
because I was now harmless and entirely in their hands, the doctors
had taken off their masks. The skull of one was completely bald and
should have reminded me of something, but I couldn't figure out what.
He had stepped back a few paces, as though to admire his handiwork,
and the smile that creased his face was like a bestial leer. From the
way he was bent I assumed he suffered from curvature of the spine.
The other one still leaned over me and, with a perverse satisfaction
in his paranoid eyes, was busily drawing lines on the space between

my chest and my navel. It occurred to me that he might be drawing lewd pictures and I smiled. After all, it was an ideal surface for such ornamentation.

When they spoke to me I don't think it was from any desire to explain themselves. Until now they had treated me like an object, but perhaps deep down they needed some appreciation of their work from me personally. The one with engraver's talents spoke: "It was for your own good," he said. "Our idea . . ." I didn't let him continue. Belatedly, I finally understood what was going on. I said: "With all due admiration for your skill, allow me to say that it is absolutely impossible for you to have ideas."

Apparently they didn't expect my impertinence. I saw their faces darken with a mixture of rage and sorrow over my ingratitude. I must admit that, although I had nothing worse to expect from them, I was afraid. I turned my eyes, seeking the nurse. She was standing by my head holding a basin with the remaining plaster. She looked at me sadly, with a kind of well-intentioned reproach, and the expression in her eyes was a lesson in patience. Before I could prepare for anything new the bald one went over to the nurse, reached his hand into the basin, and flung the first trowelful of plaster in my eyes. I felt it burning my eyeballs and in a flash the resemblance which had been bothering me all this time became clear. The doctor was the same man who had been operating the compressor. I wanted to scream from the burning in my eyes but I gritted my teeth instead. Then two vicelike fingers grabbed my jaws and forced them open. I felt my mouth filling with the thick, mushy mass of plaster. Its taste was not altogether unpleasant, but I had already begun to suffocate.

translated by Theodora Vasils

Holy Sunday on the Rock   MENIS KOUMANDAREAS

A ship tearing the heart of the night; however you looked at it,
it was like a castle in "combat readiness," every halyard a raised sword,
and the fore-topgallant sails, aiding darkness, unseen in all that was
to come. And as the darkened ship docked in dead quiet, suddenly,
from deck to bridge, there were flames, torches, and, simultaneously,
a loud, ear-splitting trumpet peal plunging the soul in anguish. And
like a curtain going up, swings came unfastened from high on the
halyards and all at once were transformed into rope ladders with
grappling irons holding onto the pier. A crowd in panoplies, spears,
and helmets began to come ashore. Whole swarms of them were land-
ing, some hanging from lines, some climbing down the rungs, running
and mouthing harsh sounds that meant one thing in their language
and another in ours. Meanwhile, the people were just standing there
silenced on the wharf; and since nobody had anticipated a war show,
at least not one played *that* realistically, it stabbed their hearts with
fear, under their capes and velvet garments. And as if meant to make
all hope vanish, the ship's flag came panting up on the high midmast
and fluttered like a death notice.

And as soon as the spectators who were in the first row of standees
felt the swords touching them, cutting into them, they cried out. A
general wailing followed, drowned by the clanging of weapons and

the beating of one shield against another as they all advanced in file continually converging in a satanic design. And those trying to escape one column, immediately fell into another, in the end hitting one another, their faces distorted by terror. Those who could slip through, and managed to escape, ran on all fours to the nearest houses. But the privileged viewers, who got their warning through their windows, had already taken care to secure their doors with bars. No matter what cries and poundings they heard, they had no intention of opening, whether for brother, child, mother, or father. The old proverb applies here: bang all you like on the deaf man's door.

The inhabitants of the Rock, however, took to their boats. But by the time they disentangled the lines and turned seaward, flaming torches hurled by the actors on the ship caught up with them, and, before your very eyes, the boats were blown up, throwing timbers and limbs about indiscriminately. And to press the slaughter into a triumph, blood spouted forth like a fountain, and voices shrieked or bellowed, each minute, each hour.

Methodically, street by street, hill by hill, the pirates, since it's time we call them by their name, poured forward, decimating the decent populace. They killed the men on the spot, carried the women into slavery, and if there was a really beautiful one, they would cut off her nipples, stick them on their spears, and then advance like real trophy bearers.

And amid the horde of warriors, these stood out: "Prisoner of the Moon," laughing stupidly and frantically, his parchment-yellow hair dazzling on the cold steel of his uniform; he caught and slaughtered as many as he could. When he saw Markos far off, running in his blue suit, he followed him like a barber who had escaped from daily routines to race a butterfly, took out a pair of scissors from his pocket, the same rusty scissors, and he stuck them in his eyes. The eyeballs fell out, white, dazed, and Markos fell prostrate and you couldn't hear a thing; you only saw the blue suit go mad.

Nearby, "White Cloud" had caught handsome Lambis, and after pulling him away from his love, he dragged him like a dirty dog, and treated him like one too, whipped him, kicked him, stripped him naked, and in a savage, blunt way outraged him horribly. The granddaddy hawk perching on "Golden Tiger's" shoulder stretched its wings and stood poised in the magnificent spectacle, which is what the piratical invasion was like in its artful staging, and stuck its beak into the tender flesh of infants, and ate the eyes of little girls, as it rushed mindlessly left and right, enjoying these tidbits.

Then along came "Doudou," even more awful than a pirate, with no weapons, or even a spear, just filed nails painted red that cut through the velvet garments and got directly to the flesh and even deeper. And she was a shameless beast, rabid, which she was even in her good moods, and she grabbed children to eat their genitals; she spat and cursed in the language of monkeys, exhibiting her buttocks that were rosy like face powder, powder puffs.

And right behind her the triumvirate "Touch-me-not, Mourner, Shiverer," one body and six legs, like a borer or scorpion, and it was as the latter that he finished off all that the others hadn't had time to kill. And they were mean like the triple-headed dog at Hades' gate and they barked unspeakable words in a foreign tongue and they destroyed with foreign insolence.

Finally, holding torches, and juggling them from one hand to another like a circus child, came "Pharaoh." Now and then he stopped to help a virgin in her blood, or to finish off some moaning child out of pity. And he seemed paler than gold, since he was the only one who kept on his uniform. Just he and the actors' leader, whom everybody called "The Ornament of the Whole Bunch."

As for this one, he wreaked havoc without joining in. Everything on him, his clothing, his hair, seemed to exude pretentiousness, reaching the furthest point that passion can know and act out. And while the joy of extermination beamed on everybody's face, rage glazed his own into a sober mask and a light radiated from his clothes as if he were performing a god-pleasing and redeeming act.

The natives—who were left and still able to move—crawled into their homes, or forced their way into other people's homes. And then the pirates began to break open the bolted doors, with their own bodies and with siege engines that they pulled like little cannon on wheels. The bars and latches were strong, a thousand years old, made by proud blacksmiths, and it took three or four bodies and one or two machines to demolish them. Where a body or machine wasn't enough, the Leader used his foot, a black foot showing through the trouser-leg, and the doors gave way. In their place was a black and terrible hole like a verse out of the Apocalypse, homeless vipers running through it, spiders brandishing their claws wrathfully, spewing poison, running on a thousand legs or legless until they reached the spasm of copulation and the end of things.

As soon as they entered the homes and mansions, and even before killing the people, the pirates gouged the life out of the furniture, cutting up holy tables and dragging and degrading the embroidery and the linen on the floor, and likewise slamming down the ancestral pictures, eradicating families back to their founders and spreading devastation to the entire family tree and its branches. All the silver, china, and even whole curtains they came onto they stuffed into sacks open like lion mouths. Plaster fell from the ceilings, a shriek rose tumultuously, trunks were left open and desecrated, the bedding was thrown off the beds, and box-spring mattresses were gored and left gaping. And everything that momentarily escaped was wiped out the next minute. With the looting came fire, and you could see the flame rearing its head and leaping from roof to roof spreading out red and devastating.

Homes burned, lives were consumed and bedridden old women and rickety old men were wasted and left to lie in plane-shavings in a lurid undoing of the flesh. The spectacle of the city was livid and red like a body bloated by foul disease and the sky dull, Stygian. It rained fire and blood incessantly and the whole scene turned dim like a lamp in its soot.

And it looked as if the huge swords of heaven had opened fire, and that all sorts of monsters were running, some on wings, some on wheels or crutches, medusas, sphinxes, lepers' wounds, and venereal diseases, and that music from the earth's center had begun, and cymbals and shambles resounded and all the other drums of horror as well. And all expected at any moment for the seventh of the heavens to be torn up and the terrible Creature blindly reigning over the blind to appear. But such a ripping open simply would not happen, because since ancient times the sky was already blunted in sorrows and knots

and ruins and only the sterile breath of destruction was heard, sowing
bereavement, lust, all sorts of condemnations unjustly meted out to
both the just and the unjust, which is why there was no real need
for that decimation to end, to diminish.

And the earth shook to its foundations, above and below the Rock,
and it pierced even to the bones of the deceased, all those who had
stayed holy and hidden, all those that the glow of destruction caused
to squeak in unspeakable lubricity, and to shiver and shake at its touch,
and to melt in sobs of reminiscing. This reached all over the insides
of the earth, on the inside of rocks, down to worms, to whatever is
darkest, foulest, and basest that this world can show.

And only Alimos hiding in a boat stood suspended with his eyes
straining in the darkness, since no one had deigned to turn his way.
Even when at a certain moment "Scourge of Conscience" seemed to
pass by him brandishing her sword, she winked slyly at him. And
now the old man, lying face down in the boat, was going through
all his pockets in the hope of finding an extra cigarette.

And while all of what I am telling now was happening, "Pharaoh,"
in an underhand retreat, was seizing a girl who had passed out on
board ship.

And when, at last, the destruction calmed and the pirates' bloody
looks were tamer, one by one, and then all together like a regular
army, they took the road back and the city stood naked in horror.
For it was now pitch-dark, and most of the torches were extinguished;
otherwise your eyes would have seen so many bodies and so many
horrors dipped in their blood and in their neighbors' blood that your
eyes would go crazy; you would lose your mind. For these kinds of
records are kept only in books and even there they are anemic, since
it is very seldom that one finds the courage to keep them right.

And it would have been a cinch for you to see the carcass of
Stavraka, the first alderman, lying in front of his mansion, which also
lay in ashes, his waistcoat undone, his cape with more gashes than the
tailor had put in it and the strangest thing, his only watch going
strong and reading half-past eight, since all this had taken place in
only half an hour.

And if you had tried you would have seen Lambis' remains, anchors, hearts, figureheads, wiped out for good, and his girlfriend nearby, untouched and in all her clothes, yet defiled.

And here they are: Kontes the merchant for one, and Kontaina and the little Kontakia, and Theodoros' Marina, and Kapsalis' Marina, and even Pantelis, Captain Michales' boy who had a newly hung little body. And all around the grownups there were the children, scattered with flowers, and they were like clouds; dreams that had gone down in melting snow and were lost in it. And there were many others, both young and old, certainly just as important, but there is no more need of this story, since all lay nameless now, and the legend deals with them.

And as soon as the destruction was really over, and those meant to be taken were taken, and those meant to leave left, a silence came on stubborner than mules. And the Rock stood upright and lonely, a fragment of the city for which we have neither a place nor even a name nowadays; it was attached to a scaffolding left to watch motionless and listen mutely. Now carrion birds awakened by the orgy of destruction were flying in circles, attracted by the offal that any time now would begin to smell. But they were in no hurry, they just made their rounds waiting for dawn, when they would start their picking.

This is roughly how it was, and how it came through the spyglass of the foreign ship, the performance staged by the actors in that little naval town that we called the Rock, on a Sunday, at eight-thirty in the evening.

translated by Stavros Deligiorgis

Traffic Lights LINA KASDAGLIS

What are you doing here in this strange world that goes on and off,
green lights—red lights,
green lights—red lights.

You don't manage to make the green lights
as you run in pursuit of lost time.
A moment, a moment in the darkness—
the red lights go on again.

What are you doing on this narrow island in the street?
Your love beckons from the far shore,
beckons and vanishes without waiting for you.
Your child has gone ahead, you call but he can't hear you—
again the red lights go on.

Whoever built a house became a window,
a large window to let the exhaust fumes in,
a naked window that lights up and goes out, lights up and goes out,
and never sleeps the sleep of the just.

Lina Kasdaglis

What are you doing in this world that doesn't know coolness and mist,
the light rain, the sudden storm, the breath of God,
what are you doing in the forest that has no leaves,
gathering plastic flowers and shapeless words under the tree trunks—
Programming, Public Relations, Expansion of Labor Enterprise.

Green lights—red lights.
The red lights go on again
but you haven't made it across and never will.

translated by Edmund and Mary Keeley

The Style of a Language and the Language of a Style   ALEXANDROS ARGHYRIOU

Il n'est pas douteux que chaque régime possède son écriture, dont l'histoire reste encore à faire. L'écriture, étant la forme spectaculairement engagée de la parole, contient à la fois, par une ambiguïté précieuse, l'être et le paraître du pouvoir, ce qu'il est et ce qu'il voudrait qu'on le croie: une histoire des écritures politiques constituerait donc la meilleure des phénoménologies sociales.—Roland Barthes

After our War of Independence (1821) the Greek state set up within the narrow boundaries of 1832, established by the Treaty of Constantinople, proceeded to evolve through a long series of inconsistencies and contradictions. The problems which the infant country faced were enormous and its means of dealing with them altogether limited and clipped. The political leaders left over from the final years of the War, having pushed aside those warriors who had exemplified and carried out the original ideas of the *Philikē Hetairia* (the secret revolutionary society), invariably proposed programs that corresponded to their own compromising and conservative cast of mind.

In keeping with this general tendency we see the granting of high official posts to foreigners, like the English general Church and Lord Cochrane, creating the basis for a deeper penetration by the foreign elements; thus the Protecting Powers are both securing their interests and becoming the determining factors in the formation of the new

169

state. Only the divergence of views between these Powers allows a slight margin for manipulation; in the beginning President Kapodistrias appears to take advantage of this. Yet, for all his diplomatic skill, even he cannot long satisfy the increasingly harsh demands of the foreigners, who rapidly undermine him and propose monarchy as the solution to Greece's difficulties. And just as Kapodistrias, in spite of his capability, experience, and good intentions, is unable to impose order on chaos (perhaps because he cannot grasp the deeper causes of internal conflict), so the situation becomes ever more confused. His assassination, though the result of a collateral event, immediately makes it possible for the Protecting Powers to impose a more strongly centralized form of government. The Bavarian Regency consists of three foreigners, whose job, as they see it, is not to participate in the building of a new country from existing resources, but rather to impose from above a set of ready-made plans. Yet the first two prime ministers appointed by King Otto on reaching his majority are also foreigners, and the installation of numerous foreign missions intrudes a foreign way of thinking into each and every manifestation of the young country's evolving life. Consequently, all roads are laid out on a mistaken plan.

The people for whose sake all this supposedly is taking place are ignored completely, while their planners and protectors take it upon themselves to do their thinking for them. In this way, however, it is not so much the freedoms of the land that have been trampled under as that, without the participation and consent of those concerned, whatever is done from now on cannot express their needs or aspirations. In such an environment the Greeks are living as second-class citizens. This race, which should be proud of having shaken off a bondage of four centuries, is not thought capable of voicing an opinion on matters concerning it. Foreigners must rule it, foreigners select the forms of government it must follow in the future. Therefore, its revolutionary fervor refuses to give way to a more constructive spirit. The words of Rhigas' patriotic hymn [1797], "How much longer, youthful fighters," are replaced by the more popular, "How much longer will the foreign locust . . ."

In the intervals between new revolutionary outbreaks some sketchy state machinery is spasmodically set up. None of the programs or methods or decisions correspond to the conditions of the land or make any attempt to develop existing precedents; study of the material at hand would require hard work and an interest that is absent. Certainly if these programs had been put forward by the country's own natural leaders an entirely different spirit would have gone into them. However, with the state machinery now in operation, all and sundry are obliged to adhere to its unfathomable laws. Each new act or program is heaped on top of all the earlier ones, confirming previous results and burning all bridges of return.

Within this framework there also comes into operation the form of language in which abstract principles are to be expressed and systematized. But what actual condition of the Greek language in those times could provide a precedent for this?

A few years before the Revolution, in the period of the Greek Enlightenment, we have a group of intellectuals working extensively together to develop and modernize the existing language of a long-subject people, with all its needs and inadequacies. Various kinds of texts in fact are written or translated in order to prepare material to meet the needs of a liberated country. The most thoroughly and clearly worked-out language form to emerge from these refining efforts, the one with the greatest influence, is that of Korais. It was considered a moderate solution, halfway between the existing spoken language and the archaizing trend. In any case it was something new, and tended toward a "purification" of the existing language, though Korais' own sense of style allowed him, in spite of his "principles," to keep all the vigor and capacity of the living tongue. The result explains the widespread diffusion of his speeches. For instance, the first proclamation by Alexander Hypselantis at Jassy (February 24, 1821), the call to arms for the uprising, is worded more or less in this spirit, while several other proclamations are in the simpler style. However, even the decisions of the Troezen Assembly are written in a language influenced by the more elaborate Phanariote tradition of Constantinople, though adhering in some significant details to Korais' standards. Naturally the language written then shows a variety of tendencies; those who use it have not grown up in a unified climate of education, nor

has the need arisen for a uniform way of writing. The need for a
single instrument of language begins to make itself felt as soon as
the scattered forces of educated Greeks come together on free territory
and, as citizens of the nation now, are ready for a dialogue with one
another.

Kapodistrias, who admires and corresponds with Korais, buys his
books and distributes them to the schools now making their first hesi-
tant experiments. A report to the Secretariat for Public Education and
Religious Matters states: "Man proceeds more rapidly and surely from
the known to the unknown; so children's learning should begin with
the mother tongue and through the mother tongue. We must therefore
plan a grammar and a dictionary of the mother tongue." We are still
in a period when the wielders of authority maintain direct contact
with their origins.

Soon after, in 1835, under the Regency, an outmoded linguistic ap-
paratus enters the service of the state machinery with the acceptance
of Armenopoulos' *Six Books on the Public Laws of Our Glorious Byzantine Emperors*. The terminology and style of language now adopted
are to affect radically the entire science of law, tied as it is to all
the state's functions. But in the prevailing climate the phenomenon
is accepted passively. In the general atmosphere of doubt as to the
value of things Greek, these despised descendants defend themselves
by exalting past glory. A whole people which daily faces its own dis-
possession would seem to have no other means of fortifying its position
or persuading that it represents that glorious past than by accepting
an archaizing language and substituting it for its own natural speech,
supposedly the product of its centuries of enslavement. It is worth
noting that both conservative and liberal elements join this backward-
looking trend.

An official language to which all consent (a force soon confirmed
by the university, which produces an intellectual scientific terminology
in the same spirit) covers every outward manifestation of the nation's
life. Solomos'* message, which was both aesthetic and cultural, has
dropped into a vacuum. The publication of his *Extant Works* by Polylas
in 1859 reaches a public by now completely apathetic.

* National poet and first important author to write in the Demotic tongue.

172

This hybrid solution to the language problem also makes possible the growth of a hybrid spirit, whose chief characteristics are bombast, insincerity, and rhetoric. Real problems are brushed aside for the sake of quibbles. The way of writing affects people's minds. The Greek race, instead of preserving its blood-stained countenance, has put on a mask; the mask begins to prompt it into a role. A people takes refuge in play-acting in order to express its feelings and ideas. But the life sources dry up, and a spirit of compromise dominates in all fields. And if art directly represents the climate of an age, insofar as its history gives us a picture of prevailing currents, it is the development of poetry in post-Revolutionary Greece that shows this phenomenon most plainly.

Poems written during the early years express a fighting spirit strongly reminiscent of the Revolution but at the same time moving toward political diction with editorial overtones: a spirit that aspires to participate in the ideological fermentation and provide moral justification to political disputes. These poets obviously believe they are serving an honorable cause, that they are the spokesmen of a people, and accomplishing a patriotic task. Behind them is a long tradition of folk poetry, but the Phanariote elegance of diction also attracts them like a magnetic pole; its whole linguistic material—just because it is unfamiliar to them—seems a fresh medium for poetry. In the beginning their style preserves much of the live feeling of speech, but gradually they too submit to the state version of the language; they think it is a national version too. Poetic language deteriorates. From warm and homely it becomes formal and artificial. It moves from an authentic spoken idiom to preciousness. As times goes on the evil spreads; the tendency to catch up with contemporary foreign literature (while the foreign presence entrenches itself ever more securely, provoking constant comparison) causes foreign artistic currents to be transplanted before the proper conditions exist for a genuine influence. From the diverse aspects of the Romantic Movement flourishing in Europe, Greek versifiers comprehend only the note of hyperbole. Emotion becomes sentimentality. The release from the restraints of formalism turns into a free-for-all with room for every kind of fad. The language in use, being neither natural nor self-renewing, becomes literally unutterable.

And yet it did have something to offer. This is what Alexis Soutsos wrote in 1832:

The Hellenes have released themselves from tyranny and bondage
and yet, instead of building a temple to their Freedom,
they raise up sanctuaries to Strife and altars to their passions,
with shameful follies justify their overlords and masters.
And Anarchy advances along streets and alleys screaming,
her right hand dealing out to us now laws, now constitutions.
Guerrillas and politicos, with impudence outstanding,
like wolves that take advantage of the hurricane and turmoil
now gobble up our revenues and strip our people naked.
Undisciplined, disorderly, the soldiers of our army
have got the bit between their teeth and dashed away like horses.
Of all these evils one's the source and cause of our dissension:
the Government is split apart in two opposing factions,
and both of them, armed to the teeth, in villages and cities
strike and are struck and done to death, and neither one is victor.
Woe to Hellas, upon the edge of precipices standing!

This is the same man who shortly before was writing about Kapodistrias' press law:

The press has freedom of expression
provided only you don't damage
state officials, civil servants,
ministers, and high court judges,
and the ministers' own cronies.
The press has freedom of expression
provided only you don't write.

"The poet's voice," K. T. Demaras writes, "weighs decisively on the country's fortunes: the daily newspaper does not exist; satire and the poets' political pamphlet, together with their various other declarations, carry out the functions later to be exercised by the leading article or the journalistic commentary."

The honesty of these writers is undisputed; the aesthetic value of their writing remains questionable. One wonders how much of their clumsiness must be imputed to themselves and how much to the general climate which nourishes them. In any case it is distressing to reflect that at this same period Solomos' work was all for nothing and calls forth no deeper echo. For Solomos' poetic conscience was fully developed from the beginning; we see him as a young man abandoning the drum-roll of his Hymns and starting on his mature work, which is free from rhetorical blemishes. A patriotic poet, he sets out to justify the nation's sacrifices from the most profound interior sources. He does not simply record events but seeks to discover their essence. He feels things, as much as he intellectualizes them. His poetic instinct helps him realize that words are not definitive entities or limited to a single meaning, but that the entire manner of putting them together is what gives substance and extends their range.

In this aspect of the Romantic Movement we must consider the slogan for the *Megalē Idea*—the Great Idea of the recovery of the lost Greek Empire with its capital in Constantinople—which is announced for the first time, perhaps cloudily but with a wide vision of Hellenism, by Ioannis Kolettis in Parliament in 1844. On the one hand this demand has taken a long time to formulate, when one considers how constricting the country's borders were; on the other it is proclaimed much too soon, before even the slightest conditions exist for putting it into effect. The historian Constantine Paparrhigopoulos will undertake to give it a theoretical guise and, with the completion of his work, reveal it in all its historical, racial, and ideological details. Anyway, the growth of historical reserach in the years after 1850 allows us to appreciate the valuable side of the Romantics as we see the *Megalē Idea* adopted by certain men whose special talent helps them discover whatever true values can still be reached through the general atmosphere of operatic grandiloquence.

Panayiotis Soutsos' manifesto of 1853, calling for the complete resurrection of the ancient Greek language, grammar and all (though the naiveté of the idea immediately evokes a counterblast from Constantine Asopios) proclaims a situation already, alas, fully established. And it will continue for two more full decades, while the university uses its authority, through the Voutsinas and Rallis poetry competitions, to confirm the trend. In any case, the Greek world at this time presents a picture of linguistic unity achieved. With the forms of language worked out, it can formulate its ideological positions, its political

thinking, and its emotional aspirations and reactions. This is of course
true only at the uppermost level of society; the foundation of the social
order floats in dense illiteracy, and whatever it perceives is clouded
by the greatest confusion. No program of education has been worked
out, nor is knowledge conveyed to the wider masses of the population,
who, despite this, dazedly sing little songs in the most formal, "purifying" Katharevousa. The current remains stronger than the force of
resistance.

Soon after, while the star of Achilleas Paraschos is at its height
and meaningless literature praised to the skies, a number of enlightened
intellectuals are beginning to become aware of the consequences of
a rigidly codified language and of an attitude that has lost all sense
of proportion. Even the university's invitation to Aristotelis Valaoritis
to recite his poems at the unveiling of the statue of Patriarch Gregory
V was an indirect confession of retreat; a dead language cannot express
live feelings. However, the artificial style of language has distorted
people's thinking to such an extent that it continues to flourish, even
after the first signs of a return to normal speech. It still distorts, still
flourishes today—and Greeks are paying a very heavy price.

From 1880 on there appear more and more examples of dynamic
new ideas motivated by a critical spirit and nourished by contact·with
reality itself. In politics this renovating urge is expressed by Harilaos
Trikoupis, and in the intellectual and cultural fields by Demetrios
Vernardakis, George Hadjidakis, and Nikolaos Politis. In criticism by
Emmanuel Roidis. In poetry by Kostis Palamas.

Significantly, in poetry this progressive trend receives its impulse
from a satirical journal, *Rambagas*, directed by two restless souls,
Kleanthes Triantaphyllos and Vlasis Gavrielides. Satire becomes the
weapon, and it is satire that reveals how radical the liberal spirit has
become. Greek liberalism seeks to disavow an attitude—dominant until
now—that has lost touch with reality. In *My Journey* Yannis Psycharis
presents the problem fully for the first time; his irreconcilable approach
expresses an entire nation's accumulated indignation and distress over
the forced survival of that attitude. Moreover, with *My Journey* the
spoken language, the Demotic, is used as an instrument of scholarly
prose; this comes at a time when even Demotic supporters defend

it in Katharevousa, unwilling to clash with a usage that is also frequently their own. This law of inertia, with its disastrous consequences, continues down to our own day.

Psycharis' lesson now finds an echo among the liveliest minds of the period (Roidis, Gavrielides, Palamas—the number increases steadily); it signals a return to the living sources of language that provide its deepest meaning. From now on it is clear that the movement favoring Demotic is a cultural current completely opposed to whatever is conventional and complacent. The new idea, however, spreads only in the upper social level and does not penetrate to any satisfactory depth, because Greeks have not yet received any solid education; instead they continue to deplete their energies in a worship of empty forms. The attack on the translation into Demotic of the Gospel and the *Oresteia*, launched by Mistriotis in the dawn of our century, incites the university students to demonstrate and riot; all this time the orientation of their studies has kept them from any serious examination of the real issues.

Palamas' *Satirical Exercises* records this situation and condemns it in the strongest terms.

Jackals and hounds and roosters of the dunghill
erect on their hind legs, the lot of them,
shoeshiners, rascals, idlers, and dandies.—
Their master sets them loose'. Congratulations!
And what would be the noble great ideals
that give them all that impetus, that charm?
"Trikoupis and his friends, the traitors, hang them!"
And the Psycharises? "Paid agents. Boo them down!"
Greece is a schoolmarm from the Arsakeion
stuffed to the gills with bookworms, pedants, scholars.
A fine site too, the Greek! No ounce of brain.
And from the cafe to Constantinople
to win the empire he wanders off;
the mouthpiece of his hookah for a weapon.

Nevertheless, while the sterile spirit Katharevousa protects still wins the battles, the first few serious groups that will initiate the drive toward a new departure are being formed in various fields.

The magazine *Noumas* has gathered together the most alert minds of the time. These comprehend the movement for Demotic in its broader sense, while the Educational Society, noting that the source of the evil is lack of education, seeks to bring about the preconditions for change. Alexios Delmouzos, Demetrios Glenos, and Manolis Triantafyllidis are the most important figures in this field. And Perikles Yannopoulos, Ion Dragoumis, and Anghelos Sikelianos are the chief exponents of a regenerative tendency aimed at bringing the nation to a point of self-understanding.

The new way still meets many obstacles; conventionality still dominates in every walk of life. And even within the Demotic Movement internal factors rob it of its force. That same idolization of formality which it so vigorously condemns has already fatally distorted the whole Greek way of thinking. For this reason several exponents of the Movement lose themselves completely in external forms, forgetting the essential matter for which they are struggling. Our literature of regional customs at this period may be in principle an attempt to return to, appreciate, and represent the roots of our national traditional culture, but in the end it impoverishes the subject. For it comes at a time when, in the development of our society, the center of gravity has shifted from the small communities to the bourgeois city. Denser, larger concentrations of population, with their resulting pressure, allow a modern current to arise in which the language question represents not so much a means of expression as a criterion for the judging of urgent questions. Language itself is the notation and recording of situations, facts, realities.

The Revisional Parliament of 1911 does, however, discuss the language question, but on a false basis and without knowledge of the facts. For want of daring or (in the case of some politicians) objectivity, it seeks to halt by legislation the very movement it had begun to develop. Although significant linguistic scholarship shows that the Demotic is not a language corrupted and vulgarized by centuries of enslavement, but the natural evolution from Ancient Greek, the legislators seek, through a special article of the Constitution, to protect the language of officialdom and keep it from slipping any closer to the language of the people: no civil servant is allowed to use it either in his work or elsewhere. Demotic Greek, which was already outside the law, is now officially declared illegal. Palamas himself, Secretary of the University, must pay for his article in *Noumas* with a month's suspension from his post.

Nonetheless, we are here in a period when Greece has entered the cycle of headlong evolutions. Conditions and the spirit they embody change rapidly from year to year as ever more factors emerge. Prejudices lose their force, and the Demotic Movement steadily gains ground. What Eleftherios Venizelos did not dare attempt in 1911, he decides to do in the revolutionary turmoil created by his clash with the Monarchy in 1917, when he entrusts the new educational policy to Demetrios Glenos. The foundations of educational reform are laid by a staff possessing all the requisite seriousness; it is marked neither by partiality nor by obsessiveness. And though the Demotic is given equal importance only in the first grades of primary school, the awakening critical spirit begins to bear fruit immediately. From this point on, educational reform alternates with phases of regression, according to the system of thinking prevailing in the political arena. The fact that Greek conservatism becomes the repository of Katharevousa, holding stubbornly to the ideological clichés of the past and identifying these with nationalism itself (a phenomenon without parallel among any European people), shows how the structure of a language can affect thinking itself. It is a case of clothes making the man.

For that reason, too, we entered a vicious circle from which there seems no escape. But problems are not solved only at the apex of the pyramid. For years conditions have been created for a demystification of the matter; a greater desire for more substantive studies and wider levels of the population becoming more aware of the realities of the time, more capable of selecting what suits its own free conscience. Just as the Demotic language used today in various sciences proves its adequacy in specific fields, so are its value and effectiveness justified by its clarity, simplicity, and directness. The preference of commercial publishers for texts written in Demotic Greek counter only to the pedantry of schoolteachers, tips the scale definitely in its favor and proves that it corresponds in fact to our feeling for our own language and our need for expression.

The attempt of the Greek state after the Revolution of 1821 to forge a language suitable to the diverse forms of life in our new country produced an instrument used quite satisfactorily by certain gifted individuals. The world-view of Constantine Paparrhigopoulos, for instance, owes much to its linguistic style. One can cite other writers whose talent kept them from taking refuge in an inflated style of writing and whose Katharevousa was reasonably structured and precise.

But the most elementary uniformity is absent from these various forms of Katharevousa; the different examples are not shades of style but simply answers to each writer's version of the "purity" or to the historical period of Greek that he has chosen looking backward for his model. This proves that even as a synthetic official separate language Katharevousa is a personal affair, not one that can be dealt with by an entire nation. The great expenditure of effort required for such an end result (an effort necessary to the philologist but superfluous in whole areas of knowledge) makes the instrument unsuitable. The colossal effort made to diffuse and learn it shows that intention was not lacking. Conversely, the resistance we have noted to a linguistic form that for so many decades has been forcibly crammed into people through teaching reveals how foreign it has been to our natural instinct for expression. The final mockery is that most of those who think they know it, ultimately use it in distorted forms. So, if even the proponents of this language cannot speak or write it correctly, what is to save it when these last props are gone? After pursuing for more than a century the vision of Katharevousa known by all educated Greeks on leaving school, it is incredible (perhaps abnormal?) that our leadership still is not discouraged. Perhaps we need a general psychoanalysis.

The drastic simplification of Katharevousa over the last fifty years is not the normal development of a living tongue when compared with any other European language during the same period. Rather, it results from the Demotic spirit constantly working against it, while the public too—facing facts with greater independence of mind—refuses ever more stubbornly to accept things passively or play a neutral role. However, we still seem unable to heed the message of statistics.

Nevertheless, the long use of Katharevousa—obligatory for the state, the schools, the press—produced a situation that has gradually debased and falsified our whole sense of language. Whatever kind of Greek may be in process of formation now is different from what it would have been if solid foundations had been laid in the beginning. But one cannot remake history. And a consequence of the distortion of our minds by language is the fact that even educated Greeks have difficulty expressing themselves. We have lost our directness of expression.

What has been dealt the severest blow in our own day is the actual style of Katharevousa. Although it seems to lie unclaimed like a foundling, without status as it were, it goes on displaying all its triumphant pompousness and tremendous pretense of gravity. This is the price the "purifying" movement must pay from now on for its indifference to the simplifying tendency of the modern age, the tendency to strip things of their facades.

If Katharevousa is still being kept alive, it is because of preservative medicines given by a state machinery accustomed to the spirit of conformity. Modern man has understood what a monstrous force is represented by that machine and how, in its rigidity and inertia, it can, indiscriminately and cynically, be made to serve black, white, or any other hue; similarly, he understands that change will begin only when that machinery itself is able to function along new lines. Personal initiative may have prepared the way in Greece, and may extend it further, but even with sympathetic (if insufficient) contributing forces, the result will never be more than partially significant. The definitive solution will come with the official and final acceptance of the Demotic by the state, when the entire machinery of government consents to express itself in the language spoken by the people it governs. The way in which this change will be brought about is a matter of tactics. First, both languages must be given equal importance in the schools. The last bastions to fall will not be the abstract theoretical sciences but the language of bureaucracy, which, written and spoken as it is by people of different levels of education, is the most inconsistent.

It is not in vain and not for mere form that the nation will make this effort. For, as contemporary linguistic studies have shown, language is neither a form nor a means, but a vital essence, consubstantial with the spirit it expresses.

It is impossible to tell when this may become known to our leadership, who find it easier to accept an already existing situation, easier not to clash with what they consider consolidated. Impossible to tell how long they will consider any change to signify a revolution. Still, one should never rule out the unpredictable in history.

In any case, the only consolation is that human beings do die off and thus life is renewed with fresh ideas, as the English historian Toynbee has written with phlegmatic but macabre logic.

translated by Kevin Andrews

The Authors

GEORGE SEFERIS 1900–1971

Born in Smyrna, 1900; family name was Seferiades. Left his native city in 1914 to study in Athens, and later in Paris, 1918–1924, where he earned a degree in law. Two years later he was appointed to the Greek ministry of Foreign Affairs. During diplomatic career served in the Greek Consulate in London, in Koritsa, Albania, and with the Greek government in exile in Crete, Egypt, and South Africa. After the war was ambassador to Lebanon, Syria, Jordan, and Iraq. Member of the Greek delegation to the United Nations in New York, 1956–57; ambassador to Great Britain, 1957–1962. Awarded Nobel Prize for Literature, 1963; other awards include honorary degrees from the universities of Salonika, Oxford, and Princeton; elected Honorary Foreign Member of the American Academy of Arts and Sciences. In 1970 the Greek government refused to validate his diplomatic passport in order for him to travel to Italy to receive a literary prize from the Italian government. Died in Athens, September 20, 1971. Seferis' principal poetic works are *Turning Point* (1931), *The Cistern* (1932), *Mythistorema* (1935), *Book of Exercises* (1940), *Logbook I* (1940), *Logbook II* (1944), *"Thrush"* (1947), *Logbook III* (1955), *Three Secret Poems* (1966). His main prose works are *Three Days at the Monasteries of Kappadokia* (1953), *Essays* (1962), *Delphi* (1962); his essays appeared in English as *On the Greek Style* (1966). He translated T. S. Eliot's *The Waste Land and Other Poems* and *Murder in the Cathedral*; several other American and European poets in a volume entitled *Transcriptions*; the Greek septuagint version of *The Song of Songs* into modern Greek, and *The Apocalypse* of Saint John. His *Collected Poems, 1924–1955*, translated into English by Edmund Keeley and Philip Sherràrd, were published in 1967.

183

The Authors

MANOLIS ANAGNOSTAKIS

Born in Salonika, 1925. Collections of poems: *Epochs* (1945), *Epochs 2* (1948), *Epochs 3* (1951), *The Sequence* (1954), *Poems 1941–1956* (1956), *The Sequence 3* (1962). Has also published a volume of critical essays entitled *Pro and Con*, and has translated *Two Odes of García Lorca* in collaboration with Kleitos Kyrou. Publisher and director of the periodical *Kritike*, 1959–1961. Other works have appeared in periodicals (*Elefthera Grammata, O Aionas Mas, Epitheorese Tehnes, Kritike, Epohes*, and others) and newspapers over the last 25 years.

NORA ANAGNOSTAKIS

Born in Athens. Essays and studies of contemporary poetry and prose have been published in the periodicals *Kritike, Nea Poreia, Endohora*. Her study on "Logbook I" appeared in the volume *On Seferis* (1961). Has translated and written introductions to the works of Roland Barthes, and of representatives of the French anti-novel Claude Simon, Michel Butor, Natalie Sarraute, Alain Robbe-Grillet, and others.

ALEXANDROS ARGHYRIOU

Born in Alexandria, 1921. For many years wrote book reviews for the periodicals *Elefthera Grammata, Politiki Tehni, Angloellenike Epitheorese, Kainouria Epohe, Kritike, Epohes*, and the newspapers *Demokratikos Typos, Hemera*, and *Mesemvrine*. Has published various studies in the periodicals *Nea Poreia, Epitheorese Tehnes, Dialogos*, and *Tahydromos*, and in the newspaper *To Vema* mainly about authors of the postwar period. Has written extensively on the poetry of George Seferis, Odysseas Elytis, Yiannis Ritsos, Nikeforos Vrettakos; on the prose of George Theotokas; on the writers of Salonika; and on Greek Surrealism. Wrote the introduction to *Anthology of Postwar Poets*, and supervised the *Encyclopedia of Contemporary Greek Literature*, never completed, for the publisher Hemera (1952).

KAY CICELLIS

Born in Marseilles. Novels and short stories written in English were published in London and New York. Her books include *The Easy Way* (1950), *No Name in the Street* (1952), *Death of a Town* (1954), *Ten Seconds from Now* (1956), and *The Way to Colonos* (1960). Her work has appeared in the periodicals *Stahys, Angloellenike Epitheorese, Tahydromos, Epohes, Ekloge*, and *Kainouria Epohe;* and, abroad, in *Encounter, London Magazine, Vogue, Harpers, Atlantic Monthly, Botteghe Oscure*, and *New Mexico Quarterly*. Received a Ford Foundation grant, 1969.

The Authors

T. D. FRANGOPOULOS

Born in Athens, 1923. Has published collections of poems: *Poems* (1953), *Poems II* (1956), *The Plans of a Journey* (1956), *The Other Poems* (1957), *Poems: A Selection* (1963), *A Private Way* (1966); and novels: *Fighting at the Walls* (1954), *Endurance* (1957), *Kapodistrias* (1959), *Ypatia* (1968). His works have been published in periodicals such as *Kritike, Diagonios, Nea Poreia, Palmos, Filoloyika Hronika, Prosperos, Stahys, Kypriaka Grammata, Epitheorese Tehnes, Nea Estia, Kainouria Epohe, Tahydromos,* and *Epohes.*

GEORGE HIMONAS

Born in Kavala, 1936; raised in Salonika. His published prose works are *Peisistratos* (1960), *Excursion* (1964), *Mythistorema* (1966), and *Dr. Ineotis* (1971).

LINA KASDAGLIS

Born in Corinth; raised and now resides in Athens. Has published two collections of poetry: *Heliotropes* (1952), and *The Streets of Noon* (1962); translations of Steinbeck's "The Red Pony" (*Nea Estia*), Mauriac's *Black Angels,* and Gide's *Pastoral Symphony.* Has contributed articles and translations to the periodicals *Nea Estia, Tahydromos, Epohes, Ios,* and *Merian;* also writes children's literature.

NIKOS KASDAGLIS

Born in Kos in the Dodecanese islands, 1928; lives in Rhodes. Has published *Gusts of Wind* (1952), a collection of short stories; and three novels: *The Teeth of the Millstone* (1955), *Kekarmenoi* (1959), and *I Am the Lord Thy God* (1961). His original works and translations have been published in *Epohes* and in other periodicals and newspapers.

ALEXANDROS KOTZIAS

Born in Athens, 1926. Has published the novels *Siege* (1953), *A Dark Case* (1954), *Lucifer* (1959), and *The Attempt* (1964), and a drama, *Furnished Room for Rent* (1962). Wrote book review column, 1961 to 1967, for the newspaper *Mesemvrine.* Has translated the works of many foreign writers, including Dostoevsky, Kafka, George Finley, Arthur Koestler, Cesare Pavese, and Robert Graves.

MENIS KOUMANDAREAS

Born in Athens, 1933. Collections of short stories: *The Pin-Ball Machines* (1962), *Salina* (1967). Has contributed to *Epohes, Tahydromos, Epitheorese Tehnes.* Translator of works by Hermann Hesse, Carson McCullers, and

The Authors

William Faulkner. The excerpt in this volume is from an unpublished short story read at the Goethe Institute (Athens), March 1968.

TAKIS KOUFOPOULOS

Born in Athens, 1927. Has published two collections of short stories, *Brief Stories* (1969), and *The Street* (1962). Has contributed to various Greek and foreign periodicals.

D. N. MARONITIS

Born in Salonika, 1929. Assistant professor of classical Greek literature at the University of Salonika until January 1968; as a classicist dealt with the *Odyssey* and the work of Herodotus. Some of his studies include *Investigation of the Style of Herodotus* (1962), *Introduction to Herodotus* (1965), *The Nostalgic Return in Various Odysseys* (1965), "The Quest and Return of Odysseus," Hellenika, no. 21 (1968), no. 22 (1969). His writings on modern Greek poetry have appeared in the periodicals *Kritike* and *Epohes*.

SPIROS PLASKOVITIS

Born in Corfu, 1917; Has published *The Bare Tree* (1952), *The Tempest and the Lantern* (1955), and *On Their Knees* (1964), collections of short stories; and *The Dam* (1960), a novel. Has written critical essays and short stories for various periodicals, including *Nea Estia, Epohes, Filoloyiki Protohronia, Nea Poreia.* Has also written for the newspapers *Eleftheria, Mesemvrine, Ta Nea.* Lectured extensively on "The Prose of Ethos" at Parnassos in 1962, and on "The Prose of George Theotakas" at the National Theater of Northern Greece, in 1967. Gave a series of literary talks on the Radio Station of the Armed Forces.

RODIS ROUFOS

Born in Athens, 1924. Under the pseudonym Rodis Provelenghios published a trilogy of novels called *Chronicle of a Crusade: The Root of the Myth* (1954), *March in the Darkness* (1955), *The Other Shore* (1958). Under his own name published *The Day of Judgment* (drama, 1957); *The Age of Bronze* (novel, 1960); *The Graeculi* (novel, 1967). Has also translated from ancient Greek Xenophon's *Hellenica* and Longus' *Daphnis and Chloe.* He has contributed to the Greek periodicals *Kipriaka Grammata, Nea Estia,* and *Epohes* and to various foreign periodicals.

TAKIS SINOPOULOS

Born in Pyrgos, 1917. Has published *No Man's Land* (poems, 1951), *Songs* (poems, 1953), *The Acquaintance with Max* (poem, 1956), *No Man's Land*

The Authors

2 (poems, 1957), *Helen* (poem, 1957), *Night and Counterpoint* (poems, 1959), *The Ballad of Joanna and Constantine* (poem, 1961), *The Making of Poetry* (thoughts on poetry, 1964). The volume *On Seferis*, 1961, includes his study "Turning Point, 1931–1961." Poetry critic for the periodicals *Simerian Grammata, Kritiki, Epohes*. Extensive contributions to periodicals and newspapers, including *Kallitehnika Nea, Filoloyika Hronika, Nea Estia, Kohlian, Poiytiki Tehni, O Ainoas Mas, Simerina Grammata, Nea Poreia, Diagonios, Kainouryia Epohe, Angeloellenike Epitheorese, Kritike, Epitheorese Tehnes, Endohora, Epohes, Tahydromos, Eleftheria, Ta Nea,* and *Mesemvrine*. Has translated many foreign poets and essayists, including Montherlant, Jouve, Farge, Miloz, Apollinaire, Emmanuel, Tzara, Bonnefoy, Alain, Eliot, and Camus.

STRATIS TSIRKAS

Born in Egypt, 1911. Since 1927 has contributed poems, short stories and articles (on Cavafy, Seferis, Voutiras, Nikos Nikolaidis, Kosmas Politis, Yiannis Beratis, Mikhail Sholokhov, Paul Eluard, Etiemble, and others) to *Panegyptia, Alexandrine Tehne, Keryx, Neollenika Grammata, Elefthera Grammata, Epitheorese Tehnes, Kainouria Epohe, Tahydromos, Hellen, Alexandrine Logotehnia, Fone, Paroikos,* and *Kypriaka Grammata*. Collections of poems: *The Fellahin* (1937), *The Lyrical Journey* (1938), *Next-to-the-Last Farewell and the Spanish Oratorio* (1946); collections of short stories: *Strange Men* (1944), *April is the Cruelest* (1947), *The Sleep of the Reaper* (1954), *Nouredin Bomba* (1957), At the Cape (1966). The novel trilogy *Ungoverned Cities: The Club* (1961), *Ariagne* (1962), *The Bat* (1965), banned in Greece from 1967 to 1970, published in French by Le Seuil, 1971, and will appear in English, translated by Kay Cicellis, published by Knopf. His book *Cavafy and His Time* awarded the Greek States National Prize in 1958. His other studies include "The Walls of a Critic and the Art of Cavafy" (1960), "Cavafy and Modern Egypt" (1963), "An Unpublished Text of Cavafy Concerning Ruskin" (1963), "A Tentative Chronology of the Life and Work of Cavafy" (1963). Has translated Stendhal, Jouve, Saint-Exupéry, and Anne Phillipe. Malcolm Lowry, Cesare Pavese, Erasmus, Grimm's fairy tales, and Aesop's fables. Published monographs on Calvos and Cavafy in the 1969 Encyclopedia Universalis. Also contributed to the volume *On Seferis* (1961). Represented Greece at the World Writers Congress in Paris (1937); in 1969 received a Ford Foundation grant.

THANASIS VALTINOS

Born in Kynouria, 1932. His short stories have appeared in the periodicals *Epohes and Tahydromos*. Also author of a narrative, *The Travels of Andreas Kordopatis*. His short story "Descent of the Nine" (1963) won him nationwide recognition. Grant from the Ford Foundation, 1970.